# Teaching Beyond the Limits

Teaching Beyond the Limits Balances the Scales
of Learning Just as the Product of the Means
Balances the Product of the Extreme

**By**

# Dr. L. Jordan Jackson

ISBN: 0-7596-8113-9

This book is printed on acid free paper.

1stBooks - rev. 02/26/02

# DEDICATION

This book is dedicated to all the known and unknown African-American and other minority students who were blamed because of their race, economic status, and the color of their skin when the education system failed them.

# TABLE OF CONTENTS

# PREFACE

This book is an expansion of my doctoral dissertation where much of the information were rejected because of the fear on the part of many professors in the Education Department of Curriculum And Instructions not wanting to know the truth concerning how many educators teaching in America's system refused to properly educate students from lower socioeconomic backgrounds. It is in higher education where no one cared or wanted to understand the many different ways students from lower socioeconomic backgrounds could be to taught.

This book was writing for the following reasons: (a) to have the public to become aware of the mis-education of students from lower socioeconomic backgrounds and the treatment implemented by teachers, administrators and school staff. (b) the importance to revolutionize the learning and teaching concept of African American and other minorities students from lower socioeconomic backgrounds who attend predominately white institutions at all levels.

Learning is an internal process. We only know it has taken place when we observe a relatively permanent change of behavior resulting from what has been experienced. One's learning style is a network of moderating variables which students prefer to learn. These are persistent qualities in the behavior of individual learners regardless of the teaching involved. Succinctly, learning style can be defined as a student's preferred way of learning. Holland observes that learning style largely determines the kinds of information students are able to acquire as well as how they can most effectively process it.

Most of the early research in learning style (before 1940) concerned the relationship between memory and oral or visual teaching methods. Research findings were conflicting. The early researchers were too preoccupied with identifying the one perceptual mode that would best increase learning. Before 1900, Cattell and Jostrow had attempted to relate differences in perceptual mode to general intelligence and learning performance, but without success.

Researcher, Jordan Jackson (1999) noted that behavior is a function of the person and environment. The interactive quality of a students's cognitive readiness, motivation, and the quality of instruction was implemented by educator, Benjamin Bloom which allow students to express their thoughts as individual. Kunjufu has written on the importance of teachers' adapting their own teaching/learning style situations to include a wide range of options ranging from social interaction to behavior modification approaches.

Many Caucasian educators and researchers frequently disagree as to what constitutes learning style and cognitive style. The term "learning style is the a preferred way of learning which is instilled in students and involve, knowledge which implies growth, change, how much growth has occurred, and what stimulates that growth in students. The term "learning style is often used synonymously with "cognitive style." But, "a learning style" is a broader term than "cognitive style." Cognitive style includes elements of implementations of the students' developed modality of acquired knowledge when is effective and can be implemented by students with understanding. An effective model of instruction needs to include elements of cognitive style, teaching style and learning style.

Perceived instructional strategies for students from both African and Caucasian –American students from lower socio-economic backgrounds and other minorities students in America's school systems are not conducive to learning.

Both quantitative and qualitative research methodologies were used for this study. The quantitative method was based on surveys pertaining to teaching strategies and what was perceived from the teachers' instructional strategies by African-American and Caucasian-American students from lower-socioeconomic backgrounds.

# TEACHING BEYOND THE LIMITS
## By
### Dr. L. Jordan Jackson

**ACADEMIC BRUTALITY IN PUBLIC EDUCATION IS AN INJUSTICE.**

**TEACHING MINORITY STUDENTS FROM LOWER SOCIOECONOMIC BACKGROUNDS BEYOND THE LIMITS IMPLEMENTING ECLECTIC PERSPECTIVES WILL RESULT IN ACADEMIC SUCCESS.**

**When teaching minority students in America's school system, teachers must understand that teaching is a choice and a privilege, and students have a right to be respected and given the opportunity to learn.**

Too many teachers have failed to educate. The teachers and students responded to 15 Likert-scale items. A Likert-scale is merely a selective form of questions seeking information concerning a given topic in search for particular information concerning a subject matter. The qualitative method contained nine open-ended interview questions for both teachers and students dealing with teaching strategies implemented from the school's curriculum and students' perceptions.

The overall difference between how teachers teach and how students perceive what teachers teach was statistically significantly different. Descriptive results revealed that there were differences between teachers and students as to what teachers claimed how they taught, how teachers implemented classroom strategies and how students perceived the implementations. Furthermore, the implementation of the school's curriculum was determined by the geographical area of the school and how the curriculum was implemented by teachers. Overall, the differences between teachers and students were statistically relative to the instructional strategies used in the classrooms.

The researcher has recommendations related to the implementations of instructional strategies for colleges and universities related to teachers' classroom instructional strategies at the elementary level before novice teachers enter schools teaching African-American and Caucasian-American students from lower-socioeconomic teaching minority students, particularly African-American students. Many educators do not understand how African-American students

ix

learn. Throughout history, it is evident that the educational system has repeatedly failed at successfully educating minority students. For example, high retention rates of minority students without retention support for keeping them back. The curriculum has also been designed for failure, it lacks an inclusion of cultural differences in learning styles of African-American and other minority students. It also fails to acknowledge equities between minority and majority students. In addition, teacher education programs have totally repudiated the contributing of minorities to American society. Curriculum fails to address the needs of minority students; it fails to provide inclusive instructional strategies that provide meaningful experiences for minorities. Thus, the learning process of minority students is a critical issue worthy of scholar concern.

America's educational system has a legal and moral obligation to educate all minorities.

Socioeconomic dynamics throughout race in America, depict students who are considered not favorable when it comes to education at the elementary level; they are, African-American, Caucasian-American and other minority students from lower socioeconomic backgrounds in America school system. When the National Commission on Excellence published its well-known report, A Nation at Risk (1983) it did not include the At Risk Caucasian-American Students from lower socioeconomic backgrounds along with the African-American students and other minorities with the same status. This means that the piece of the puzzle has been found when it comes to students at risk.

The infrastructure of our socioeconomic educational system at the elementary level is presently deteriorating before our eyes by a rising tide of incompetent educators who are threatening the future of many students from lower socioeconomic backgrounds. Many of these same educators have attempted to impose on America's mediocre performance in the elementary classrooms that exists today as some type of war against students from countries such as Japan and the Soviet Union, but they can save the drama. The classroom performance by African-American, Caucasian-American and other minorities students from lower socioeconomic backgrounds are at risk because of incompetent educators and a bureaucracy that interferes with the education of these less favorable students.

Students at risk at the elementary level are indeed at risk because the educational system has allowed far too many professionals such as: psychologist, philosophers, and other psychos who use the school system as a dumping ground presenting information which has nothing to do with preparing the minds of these students for the future, plus the educators at present are not preforming in the classrooms as they should as educators. Students from lower socioeconomic backgrounds are a fast-growing segment of the school population, Blacks, Whites and other minority students from lower socioeconomic backgrounds are without educational opportunities. The lack of these educational opportunities will lead to individual economic dependence ultimately without strength or survival. The current education, economic, and social condition of students of lesser wealth at the elementary level is caustic, and the outlook for their future seems desolate.

The inclusion of students from lower socioeconomic backgrounds in school reform was never intended. In the rush to create the "new curricula," few stop to ask what effect these reforms might have upon the overall pattern of public schools, or if these academic products would become widely accepted. What kind of society would result if the scholar-reformers were successful in achieving their educational objectives and would these objectives benefit all students? Parents from lower socioeconomic backgrounds in America have distrusted the centralized educational planning, (Jordan-Jackson, 1999). They fear it as a characteristic of totalitarian system and look to the autonomy of neighborhood school board as the bastion of democracy as the protector of the community school. But is this working? One might ask, what are the true intentions of the school board and who monitor the school board when it comes to educating all students?

In the late 50's early 60's the launching of the Sputnik inspired the science curriculum. It revealed something about the perils of curriculum innovation, but at the sometime, educators were leaving the schools by the hundreds to enter the world of industry for higher paying salaries. This closed the door for competent educators who left the schools unprotected for incompetent educators to enter the school's education system and plan school curricula for students without a clue as to how to teach them. At this time it is difficult to remove these incompetent educators who are coming into the school system to claim its victims who are still students from lower socioeconomic backgrounds. This act of incompetency has allowed the educational system to use every ideology and theory to nihilis and annihilate the capabilities of these students without the creation intellect of critical thinking (Dows, 1960).

If all students were included in curriculum innovation there would be the kind of curriculum planning that Bernard Bell had proposed the creation of intellectual elite, or would the result be that all students learn "how to think," as Arthur Bestor had envisioned? How would the reforms relate to the preparation for democratic citizenship that dominated the thinking of the progressives or the practical training called for by the proponents of "life-adjustment" education?

Unfortunately, in their urgency to close the "educational gap" with some well-designed courses, few of the new reformers took time to explore these broader philosophical questions or to consider the social and political ramifications of their actions.

The failure to articulate a clear social vision was in time to prove troublesome in a society deeply concerned with societal as well as the function of the schools that include all students. There is a need for innovative changes in the school curriculum which value the approach to thinking. As a college instructor, I was very vocal and taught for several years the concept of "Life-Adjustment Education." I charge the schools with failing because they had given up on the primary goal of a liberal education, to teach students how to think. I think that a rigorous intellectual training, should be the first requisite of a liberated individual and most important protection for a free society. The most damaging factors to the educational system is the inter locking directorate, and government bureaucrats, who monopolize the administration of public schools which have placed an iron shield separating schools from the scholarly community. This is the same as separating the grassroots from the political elections.

The question is do we as educators really want to teach our students to think independently and how to explore the human condition in all open-ended ways?' Are we as educators prepared to teach beyond the limits to what is described as, "the perfectability of intellect" for all students and not just for the elite? Teaching beyond the limits consists of the approach to thinking independently in the classroom, hands-on experience such as; measuring, observing, with questions and positive reply from teachers, hands-on experiences done in field work, analyzing, discussing research application, and presentation in the classroom through class participation. There are values to be considered when it comes to teaching students from lower socioeconomic backgrounds. When it came to teaching students from lower socioeconomic backgrounds in today society values were considered by very few teachers. At one time values were the characteristics of the educational system. These values constitute what one value means to other values and schema, their notions of learning about their values and what one ought to value (Jordan Jackson, 1999).

Education has within its definition many fundamental idiosyncrasies that mean many things to many people when it comes to students in elementary and higher education. The unawareness of a higher authority in teaching is to teach toward understanding and acceleration among all students. Many educators are not aware of this from the educational perspective; therefore, in order to make a creative contribution to teaching a discipline, instructors must have acquired knowledge of the discipline. Under the umbrella of all white institutions of learning, many professors teach at all levels without having the required knowledge of the discipline. Without such knowledge, educators risk discovering what is not known to them as educators and find themselves faking the discipline. Without such knowledge of the discipline, many professors are placed in learning institutions placing students' fates in jeopardy. Therefore, without knowledge on the part of professors, it is difficult for students to assess problems in the discipline which result in unfair judgment on the part of students.

In Politics, according to Paulo Freire, education apprehend subjectivity and objectivity in their dialectical relationship of understanding, that is to say, both the promise and the limitations of what he calls "consientization" —trying to focus on his efforts, he has turned himself into "a tramp of the obvious, becoming the tramp of demystifying conscientization." In playing the part of this tramp, Freire claims one should learn how important the obvious becomes as the object of critical reflection."

Paulo Freire form of teaching is to observe, and observe again the theory, practice and methods that can be derived from the dialectic relationship. Nothing in the field of literacy theory is more important than observing and observing again at the role of an awareness of awareness, of thinking about thinking, of interpreting man's interpretations, (In other words analyzing what is being taught and discussing it in its entirety).

Unlike my experience, first as a college student, I had to working harder and performing my tasks better than many of my white college classmates to secure recognition; this was not my experience in my early educational career. I came from a predominately segregated background, but I attended all predominately white colleges and universities. Out of the hard and unusual struggle throughout my college and university years. I was compelled to pass without directions from many of my university professors, I received strength, and confidence unlike my white college classmates where pathway was comparatively smooth by reason of race. From this point I present my personal experiences as a college instructor.

# INTRODUCTION

In today's society with racism, discrimination and internal biases, there is a need for multiculturalism. Society's prejudices and stereotypes are often reflected in schools causing minority students to create a vision of the future in their own way to avoid or reverse the cycle of failure.

Educators must find solutions to eliminate the impact of lower expectations, by creating cultural curricula, which will create school success and achievement for minority students. Often, minority students do not achieve at their fullest potential because of low expectations. They feel that the educational system in America does not include them as part of the mainstream and they are not respected nor appreciated, nor is their culture acknowledged.

In efforts to provide a multicultural education, one must first examine structural factors within the school system that inhibit diversity. Secondly, one must examine cultural issues including mutual accommodation, interdisciplinary lessons, and inclusive strategies of internal biases. Finally, one must examine and attempt to overcome internal biases.

Structural factors in schools involve curricula, tracking, discipline, and staff development. There is a need to involve parents, teachers, students and communities into curricula planning. In many cases where over fifty five percentage of the student body is minority, there is a negative impact which introduces tracking. Staff development is the most serious aspect of changing structural factors. If a school system is successful in recruiting a diverse staff, all other changes toward a multicultural education will follow if this particular staff collaborates for positive change, if not, all efforts will be in vain. The aim of staff development should be to search continually for culturally responsive strategies that will motivate and inspire students.

These propose differences that are sometimes (a) beyond control, but, not beyond awareness various cultures cannot be mandated, it must be cultivated through study, reflection, and action.

It is imperative that the curriculum includes direct experience of the home and communities in which the students live. Teachers should shape instruction and collaborate in the development of instructional materials based on their experience in multicultural education. Teachers must determine what motivates minority students and discover how to enhance their sense of well-being in school through inclusive strategies.

Low achieving students often become permanently segregated in groupings or tracks. Determinations of low achievement are not necessarily reliable. Mis-diagnose of students' academic abilities happen all too often when ethnic or linguistic features are interpreted as signs of low ability. Segregation in lower-track groups carries a stigma that may lead to certain students' being labeled "dummies," not to mention the more limited curricula that are sometimes offered such groups.

Schools should consider using heterogeneous groupings, such as cooperative and team learning. They should also consider using flexible and temporary ability-group arrangements. Teachers should respect the student's cultural/linguistic backgrounds and communicate this appreciation to them in a personal way. Academic programs should encourage students to reflect and build on their experiences, and at the same time expose them to unfamiliar experiences, and ways of thinking. The assumption, expectations, and ways of doing things in school are made explicit to minority students by teachers who explain and model these dimensions of academic learning.

Internal biases and stereotypical ideas about the capabilities of a child who belongs to an ethnic group will detract from an accurate assessment of the child's real educational problems and potential. By focusing on family deficiencies, educators may miss the strengths of the cultures from which many disadvantaged students come.

The adverse consequences of these biases include: (a) low expectations for what these students can accomplish in academic work; (b) failure to examine carefully what the schools do that exacerbates (or facilitates the solution) these learning problems; and (c) mis-diagnosis of the learning problems these students face.

Realizing that a child will bring to school speech patterns, cognitive predispositions, and behavioral patterns that do not match the way things are done in school. These students must learn the culture of the school while they are attempting to master academic tasks. While recognizing that there may be gaps in disadvantaged students' experience, the educator builds on their experience bases and at the same time challenges the children to expand their repertoires of experiences and skills. This perspective gains support from a decade or more of cognitive research and related theories of learning that portray the learner as an active constructor of knowledge and meaning rather than a passive recipient of information and skills. The students feel that they are a part of the culture of the school.

# CHAPTER I

# TEACHING IS A CHOICE AND A PRIVILEGE

The more one learns the more one realizes one does not know and therefore, one must study more. I have taught at the elementary and college levels and realized after reading the works of bell hooks and Gloria Billings; I was totally surprised that I had commonalities with them at both levels and was inseparable. I found that I teach beyond the limits to students who are poor and falsely labeled having a learning disabilities.

Students who begin life in devastating poverty are at a huge disadvantage when they enter kindergarten, have a shortage of resources that deem them relentlessly through every stage of the educational process. By the time they reach third grade they are already falling far behind through no fault of their own. According to a report from <u>The Carnegie Foundation,</u> over twenty-percent of poor students in America come to school unready for learning. The Carnegie Foundation reported that students at the kindergarten level arrive at school absolutely unprepared to learn. Now, these findings are totally contradictory to Jawanza Kunjufu and Jordan Jackson's findings. Students at the kindergarten level come to school prepared and ready to learn, they bring with them enthusiasm and much zeal.

In reality poor students do not share an equal chance to benefit from the opportunity provided by schooling; this is because they are poor and research is mostly done on poor students and their families. Poor elementary students, according to many biased researchers, find reasons for school failure lacking in the essential requirements for good health, physical safety and proper mental and social development. These poor students are much more likely to have higher rates of developmental and learning disabilities. These findings stem from what many biased researchers find as inadequate prenatal care that poor mothers receive which significantly increases poor students risks of having learning disabilities as they grow up. For poor students, black or white, poverty is a key to a roadblock to a poor child's education. You see this is the type of information that has poisoned the educational system in America, and the results are the birth of a failing nation.

Throughout most of the introduction and during my experiences as an elementary teacher and college instructor my exact sentiment while teaching at these levels, students must be taught from a classroom which exemplifies an open and comfortable atmosphere based on trust, support, acceptance, and mutual respect. Students must feel that their participation is valued by other students and most importantly, by teachers and professor. Since there is no one set rule as to how to teach students at any level because teachers and professors are dealing with people and must teach according to individuals modalities, because all students can learn even if they are adults. Its's just a matter of finding the right strategy, or strategies to use that will be effective. Teachers, professors, and instructors must first take into consideration the discipline being taught, the reason for teaching it, and must firmly be to a discipline, professors only need one strategy for introduction and that strategy is to tell the students what the discipline is about, and then teach the discipline in depth seeking comprehension of principles, logic, theories, and rules. Professors must first find the right strategy or strategies to convey the materials in its entirety. It takes the right strategy, which is the essence for adult students to learn from certain learning styles.

The term learning styles loosely refers to preferences for some kinds of learning activities over others understanding learning styles, the difference among people in attitude, values, and approaches. Students beginning to learn which provide the basis for developing the class activities and assignments needed to teach college students at the freshman level so that the professors can understand fully the need of all college students especially freshmen.

Good professors facilitate a learning process. Instructors, professors and teachers who are described as good, permit students to pay attention for long periods of time with less effort and take much of the onus off the students' studies. By transforming studies from work to a recreational active process is called, motivational teaching at the college or university levels. To be an effective professor, organizing materials is important when teaching the discipline which makes it easier for relationships as well as isolated facts.

Teaching beyond the limits from a black perspective on a predominantly controlled white learning institutions, is a struggle. Although these educational institutions are where Black instructors have strong analytical skills that are under scrutiny by white administrators when teaching white students. Black and white instructors who teach Black Studies must walk a thin line when teaching some white students.

My experience teaching in a 99% white classroom during the fall semester of "99" where I presented the works of bell hooks' essay on women liberation presented a problem for many white students. These students rejected the material, refused to read it and reported me as a college instructor for presenting this material. This discipline taught by a black instructor had a tendency to think and talk in a manner which shifts attention to personal experiences combined with the discipline for further comprehension created a problem for white students; whereas, some white instructors choose what portion to teach from the discipline which satisfied white students. By teaching at the college level, I take into consideration that I'm standing before adults and these adults must be respected at all times; understanding that the telling of one's personal story provides a meaningful example and a way for people to connect. I have experienced the same as hooks has in her classroom. I consider the classroom as the place for critical thinking and critical thinking should be allowed without the fear of instructor scrutinizing students, resulting in grade attack. For example, as a college instructor, I have experienced the agony from both Black and White students who expressed to me their concern in the way they are treated by many professors, the same as hooks. I also struggle to educate for emancipation in the classroom at the college level, which is the process where I find enormous stress among students, particularly students who are labeled with a learning disability, but many students at the freshman level are unable to see how to apply it in their daily lives. In my opinion professors must understand that knowledge which can not apply to everyday life is worthless; students should be taught information that can benefit them in life. This knowledge must begin in the early grade levels, not at the college level. If this knowledge does not present itself by the time students reach college it maybe too late for some students. In most cases it is too late, but, not difficult, or impossible, to be presented and accepted.

With the explanation in today's society on issues of pedagogical oppression, questions are put to test. Will the oppression come to a full fledged emancipation? How will society learn to defend itself when education has been denied for so long by the dominate masculine culture? How can Black instructors supercede and accomplish a innovative movement in education when supremacist White females still have rage in their hearts and minds against women of color? This relates to White women as an authority on Blacks as White women writers and teach Blacks students.

In my classroom, it is important for me to define the term engagement, to identify what is meant when it is said that a course will be taught from a Black professor's perspective. Often the initial explanation about pedagogy will have a serious impact on the way students experience a course. In my class there is resentment by some students toward me because I do not lecture, but allow students to discuss, analyze, synthesize, apply knowledge, and evaluate, topics.

Well, my belief is the classroom is a place where experience constitutes uniqueness of self-expression, where students express their freedom of speech which is a significant aspect of the process of acquiring knowledge, but, if they are not familiar with this type of classroom activity then this can not be accomplished, they are denying themselves of an education that falls in the category of missing class and refusing to be educated.

Missing class is denying one-self of learning is the same as a professor denying a student the right to be educated. Another import issue is class participation. I give students respect unlike some professors, this is my way of giving students respect unlike my colleagues both male and females. To me, class participation from a Black perspective is a movement from the norm to emancipating classroom politics in higher education.

Teaching from a Black perspective is an aim to transform society by eradicating patriarchy and ending undesired oppressions, challenging the politics of the domination on all fronts. In order to innovate white pedagogical classrooms on college campuses, professors who teach must abandon ties to traditional ways of teaching. This effort is difficult when white female professors courses are often viewed by dominating males as not seriously academic because of its contents of personal substances discussed. The same conclusion is evaluated toward Black Studies on college and universities campuses. To me these thoughts should extent themselves valued, not by the dominating white male, but, by every means of the educational system to the point where all professors should extend themselves to the services of others through their teaching. For example, from my perspective, classrooms should not be a place where one must struggle for acceptance, or where visible acknowledgment of alienation is the norm in contemporary colleges and the place where many Black students' careers are in jeopardy without recognition.

I can confirm what hooks states, "As an educator, I know that my colleagues should recognize the value of my thoughts, but, I know they don't. Because I value what I teach.

Students who are not taught properly at the elementary level will experience difficulties in the future. There has been always a national concern about the extent to which students in elementary schools are performing and representing academic failure of elementary school. More specifically, African-American, Caucasian-American and other minorities students from lower-socioeconomic backgrounds are becoming increasingly disinterested in learning at the elementary levels. Expert such as Epstein & Komrita (1971): Billings (1992); Waxman, Wang, Linvall, and Anderson (1988) report that the relationship which determines the rate of students' failure or success in school depends, in part, on how curriculum and instructional strategies are implemented during classroom activities in relationship to the learning styles of students. Additionally, there are several school-based contextual variables that have been frequently cited as being related to socioeconomically challenged students, that is, lower-socioeconomic African-American, Caucasian-American and other minorities students at the elementary levels. They include: (a) teachers' expectations,(b) students' learning styles,(c) student's preferred learning styles, (d) school curriculum, (e) cultural relevance, and (f) attitudes among teachers toward students from lower-socioeconomic backgrounds (Grant, 1992). Grant continues to elaborate that the work between Caucasian teachers and lower-socioeconomic backgrounds of African-American, Caucasian-American and other minorities students at the elementary level seem to indicate that these students are mentally turned off and psychologically shut down their zeal for learning if conditions for learning are not conducive to their learning styles. Since the passing of the bill to integrate schools in the deep South within the United States, African-American, Caucasian-American and other students from lower socioeconomic backgrounds have been considered as educationally disadvantaged, which currently is being reported as being socioeconomically challenged. In 1994, The Journal of Negro Education reported a study that consist of African-American students in inner-city schools of New York City (Gibbs, 1987) showing that 41% of African-American and 6% of Caucasian-American students from lower-socioeconomic backgrounds at the elementary levels were characterized as having learning disabilities, poor performances, and high dropout rate. Since the 90s, the percent is much higher (Jordan, 99). Furthermore, over 50% of teachers in the public school were Caucasian-American teachers who interacted with these types of students without teaching them for academic success. Irvine (1990), in her Synthesis of Students and School Failure, suggests that the educational system reflects the values of African-America, Caucasian-American and other minority students from lower-socioeconomic backgrounds. These types of students remain disadvantages because their socioeconomic backgrounds are incongruent with cultural pattern from those of middle-and upper-class teachers. Therefore, depending on the socioeconomic backgrounds and the culture of African-American, Caucasian-American and other minority students, these factors play a role in the quality of education they receive during their elementary school years. This role is based on: (a) values, (b) goals, and (c) beliefs that are unique to those students. There is one important note teachers should understand before entering the classroom and that is, the aspect of cultures reinforce specific patterns of behaviors that help these groups of students to adapt and survive in this environment while, at the some time, maintain the salient characteristic of culture relevance. This means culture matters when it comes to teaching students from cultures other than that of the teacher's. Irvine (1992) states that the concept of cultural differences and variations in environment are typified by the norms and expectations of American society. Furthermore, lower-socioeconomic minority students are experiencing a new set of demands for which they have not learned the social behaviors associate with the culture of some schools they might be attending that are located in suburban neighborhoods. However, in 1991, Irvine states that no piece of educational research has generated as much attention among both the lay and the professional education community as the Rosenthal and Jacobson study, "Pygmalion in the classroom." Rosenthal and Jacobson's research popularized the concept of teacher expectations as self-fulfilling prophecies, generating fifteen years of replications, critiques, subsequent refinements and the development of the ways educators view the relationship of educational expectations and students achievement. Their work took place in a lower-social-status elementary school in New York City suggesting that teachers' expectations play a major role in students' success or failure in school (Williams,

1945). Additionally, Cooper's (1985) "Expectation Communication Model," is based on the ideal that backgrounds and abilities lead teachers to display behavioral differences toward students with different expectations about academic performance and classroom contexts are influenced by the amount of control teachers have over classroom interaction in the classroom setting. According to Cooper, students are influenced by the amount of control teachers have over the classroom interaction in the classroom setting.

Moreover, school curriculum also plays a central role in teachers' behaviors and their expectations in relation to the content that is mandated to be taught in a school's curriculum. Now, public and private education in America can be credited with great achievements, but, there is a functional literacy that is ineffective for students who are at an academic disadvantage on the national level aspect of communication. This functional literacy is the cultural aspect communication. To be culturally literate is a process with basic information which gives one the privilege to communicate. Culture literacy should not be confined to just one culture or vaguely understood by other cultures when presented. Cultural literacy in America should constitute the only means to assure an opportunity for academically disadvantaged students. It will combat the social problems that have condemned these students to remain poor and illiterate which is an unacceptable failure for those concerned, Jordan Jackson (1999). During two decades (i.e. 1960-70 of social science research in compensatory education, researchers interpreted poor school performance of culturally deprived" (i.e. African-Americans, Caucasian-American and other minorities from lower-socioeconomic backgrounds) learners as long attributable primarily to poor home preparation for the school experience (Deutsche, 1964). Deutsche states that the culture of students is an important component to the academic success or failure of students in school. The epitome of this viewpoint is expressed by Murray and Smythe (1966) who list more than sixty separates psycho-educational "deficits" associated with the culturally disadvantages that defines the Zeitgeist the notion that stylistic differences should be reinterpreted as psycho-educational deficits, as value-neutral traits, or even "strengths of culturally deprived" learners. Th appearances of empirical support for "cultural" differences in learning characteristics gave strength to a growing waves of "Multiculturalist" and "Afrocentic" approaches which began to be evident in education and social science literature in more recent years (Friby, 1992).

## TEACHING BEYOND THE LIMITS IS TEACHING BLACK WRITERS LITERARY WORKS BUT NOT FROM ANY ENGLISH DEPARTMENT

In today's society, there is a need for all Black writers to enter the mainstream of Eurocentic college and university curricula. It is imperative to the reformation of race relations and multiculturalism to depict subcultures within the Black culture (Davis, 1994). When Black writers are taught on college and university campuses these works are taught from the English Department which limits the importance of the study by Black instructors as well as the students. Black Studies in America started mostly after protests and demands that fit the first type of pressure. But in many learning institutions, particularly White institutions, these courses would become attached to the larger program of the English Department without a specific role in curricula development. In this case there is a control of the teaching. Rather than have a separate department, this course is kept incarcerated just as many Blacks are in society. It is imperative for Black instructors to inform Black students and others who are interested in Black writers for race relations and muliticuturalism to depict subcultures within Black America culture from a Black perspective.

Throughout American literary history Black writers in general have been ostracized and separated from mainstream literary works. White society has constantly tried to segregate Black women's works from those of White writers. The study of Black writers is of essential, especially Black women's work in America's which is described as an outsider and is a denied culture even on predominately white colleges and universities. Many elementary school teachers and college and universities professors do not teach beyond the limits. They hide the writings of Blacks in the English Department curricula for fear of Black and White students will learn of these great writers. This is why these works are hide in the English Department and not interdisciplinary aspects such as: Black History, Women Studies, and, Sociology Departments. To teach this discipline from an English Department is just another way for White society to continue to keep many interested students from learning the true history of the African-American's literary works which includes the history and hardships of those who are described as inferior to Whites in America.

# CHAPTER II

# MANY TEACHERS HAVE LOW EXPECTATION FOR MINORITY STUDENTS FROM LOWER SOCIOECONOMIC BACKGROUNDS

If teachers use appropriate strategies, lower-achieving minorities students can perform with the same frequency of participation as others students classified as middle- and upper-socioeconomic backgrounds.

In general, research on teachers' expectations is clear. The images that teachers and other educators have about minorities students at the elementary level in inner-city schools have major influences on student success. For example, if teachers believe that a student's intellect is low, teachers will adjust their teaching levels.

Jordan, 1998 indicates that teachers who interact positively with students from middle- and upper-class situations do so by challenging them on an intellectual base, calling upon them often in the classroom.

Ogbus (1992) reported that minorities both African-American and Caucasian-American students from lower-socioeconomic backgrounds, even though they have made some gain in academic performance to lag behind their African-American and Caucasian-American from middle- and upper-class cohort groups.

Many teachers fail to mode behavior reflecting courtesy and respect toward students from lower socioeconomic backgrounds. Some teachers are rude and put discipline above respect. Students should feel that their teachers respect them. If respect is given, respect is received. Teachers who teach in inner-city schools are not prepared to teach in suburban schools; (Jordan Jackson 1999). According to Jordan Jackson, 1999, teachers gave less direction to students from lower socioeconomic backgrounds, criticize their students more, asked practically no questions for students' understanding of subject matters and accepted for clarified students' ideas less. These teachers behavior related negatively toward students' academic achievement. This has been confirmed by Irvine (1992) that low academic achievement was related to withdrawal on the part of the students and criticism on the part of teachers. While observing a pre-kindergarten class for one year, Jordan-Jackson discovered that teachers held high expectations of students who were from middle and upper classes, but those students from lower status class, teachers had no expectations.

From these teachers there frequency of verbal hostility or reprimand from teachers all related negatively toward to students achievement. Teacher praise can affect students' achievement at the elementary levels. It has been observed doing much of my research that students at pre-kindergarten, First, and Second grade level, teachers who communicated and listen to their students held high expectations. When visiting classrooms where students were from lower socioeconomic backgrounds teachers held low expectations. Teachers had thoughts that the low-expectancy students "had no idea of what was going on in the classroom." These teachers inhibited students from verbalizing and thought they had not learned anything. The results from this study found that teachers who are incompetent will place the blame on innocent students because the teachers themselves were incompetent and were from lower socioeconomic backgrounds themselves. Many schools use hidden curricula, designed to fail students who are from lower socioeconomic backgrounds.

The Jean Anyon and Ray Rist (1981) study provides an example of how a hidden curriculum operates. They interviewed teachers and principals in four elementary schools in one school district. They discovered that the curriculum objectives were the same for all students. However, the hidden curriculum in those schools provided drastically different experiences for students from various social backgrounds. For example, instructional activities in the classrooms were different in relationship to the students' social backgrounds. Billings (1990) states that all children can learn, but many teachers do not realize that students do not learn at the same rate or by the use of the same instructional techniques and learning styles. Given the diverse learning styles that African-American, Caucasian-American and other minorities students bring to the classroom, it seems that colleges and universities should consider alternative ways to train teachers when dealing with African, Caucasian-American and other minorities students from lower-socioeconomic backgrounds for academic success in the public schools. Moreover, Hamilton and Gingress (1981) indicate that teachers will interact with, call on, praise, and intellectually challenge students from middle- and upper-social backgrounds more often than students from lower- and poor-social backgrounds. How teachers implement instructional strategies in the classroom sets the tone for the process of learning as well the fate of a child future.

Instructional strategies in standard elementary curriculum guides seem to vary little in relationship to a school's location, social backgrounds and race of its student body, and students' ability levels. One could assume that because mandated courses and instructional strategies are similar, students (regardless of their race or social backgrounds) receive the same instructional strategies. This assumption, of course, is unfounded. The stated curriculum does not discriminate, but the hidden or latent curriculum does. The hidden curriculum is unstated, but influential. Knowledge, attitudes, rules, rituals, values, and beliefs are transmitted to students through structural polices, processes, formal content, and social relationships of schools (Ogbus, 1978). Theories of teaching styles should be taken with caution.

Boutte (1992) asserted that some teachers hold the belief that African-American and Caucasian-American students, especially those from lower-income homes, are not capable of performing well in the classroom in the inner-city schools. As a result, teachers may inadvertently convey lower expectations of African-American and Caucasian students from lower-socioeconomic backgrounds. Where some students receive the message of lower expectations, they lose their motivation to learn. For this reason, experts believe that too many educators have failed at educating African-American and Caucasian-American students from lower-socioeconomic backgrounds. Many educators also do not understand how African-American and Caucasian-American students learn because of their socioeconomic, historical, cultural background, and the many different learning styles that they bring into the class (Ogbus, 1992; Dunn, 1990; Comer, 1992; Kunjufu, 1990; Hales, 1993).

Furthermore, studies have indicated that teacher expectations become self-fulfilling prophecies over time (Brophy and Gild 1997; Goldenberge; Rist, 1970; Smead 1986). The phenomenon of teacher expectations is identified in the research as an influential factor in determining how much is learned by students. For example, many teachers do not think that African-American and Caucasian-American males can achieve as well as African-American and Caucasian-American females from lower-socioeconomic backgrounds. These expectations for learning could be related to the preconceived notions of teachers teaching African-American and Caucasian-American students who lack the knowledge of African-American and Caucasian-American culture from lower-socioeconomic backgrounds.

Other findings related to academic success in school for African-American and Caucasian-American students from lower-socioeconomic backgrounds were reported by Holly & Keithley (1991), indicating that this is a connection between the gender of the child and the relationship to the teacher's expectancy. Teachers are more likely to overrate the abilities of African-American and Caucasian-American girls rather than males because girls are quieter, girls seem to listen more and read and write better than males. Therefore, there is a perceived negative atmosphere among African-American and Caucasian-American males when it comes to Caucasian-American teachers who teach African-American and Caucasian-American males from lower-socioeconomic backgrounds.

African-American male students and Caucasian-American male students from lower-socioeconomic backgrounds are considered disruptive by teachers of European descent when expressing their analytical views in the classroom. However, African-American and Caucasian-American students from middle- and upper-class levels, in contrast to students who are not considered disruptive in class, are usually influenced by teacher's expectations. Studies conducted by

Sadker & Sadker (1986) revealed that equal learning opportunities are frequently denied by both males and females in their expectations of the two genders. Bennett & Bennett (1994) conducted a study in which two-hundred-and-fifty elementary education schoolteachers, half of whom were male and half of whom were female, were asked to measure their attribution of student success or failure in relation to gender-associated behaviors.

Brophy and Good (1974) and Winfield (1986) found that when teachers have low expectations for certain students of African descent and poor Caucasian descent they perceive them as low-achievers, called on them less frequently during class discussions, gave less encouragement, and gave less attention to them. Babad & Taylor (1992) and McAllister (1990) reported that teachers seldom called on low-achieving African-American and Caucasian-American students from lower-socioeconomic backgrounds who were more likely to provide very little feedback to them.

# CHAPTER III

# EDUCATORS' THEORIES OF TEACHING AND LEARNING STYLES

In theory the masturation of modalities will give incentive and task structures that increase the academic performance of students.

The author compared four-hundred students using various learning modality development methods at the elementary level in the Southern portion of the United States. The author found that the masturation of students' do not always enhance academic performance. In further analysis of the research, the author compared differences in task instructions and incentive. The Jordan Jackson study also found that learning styles used modality incentive structure working one on one instead of groups to achieve goals most consistently had a positive impact on minority students' achievement.

According to Billings (1992), many African-American scholars have argued that they are in agreement with the critical theorists about schools as a battleground in the struggle for power and the exercise of authority. The failure of these theorists to examine adequately the special historical, social, economic, and political role that race plays in the United States makes their argument less than complete for improving the educational lives of African-American students.

Many African-American scholars have begun to look at specific cultural strengths of African-American students and the ways that some teachers leverage these strengths effectively to enhance academic and social achievement. Scholars such as hooks, Jordan-Jackson, Billings, Hale-Benson and Gibbs have identified cultural strengths that African-American students bring with them to the classroom which are rarely recognized by their teachers. For example, many white scholars look carefully at language communities suggest that schools placed little value on what is termed the "nonstandard English" that African-American students bring to school. Even though that language is rich, diverse, and useful in both community and work settings the nonstandard English is still not acceptable.

Irvine has suggested that what happens between African-American students and their teachers represents a lack of cultural synchronization and the teacher's responsiveness relates to other factors that inhibits African-American students' school achievement, including the "prescriptive ideologies and prescriptive structures that are premised on normative belief systems. "Billings introduces cultural relevance" to her audience which moves beyond language to include other aspects of students and school culture. Culturally relevance teaching uses student culture in order to maintain it and to transcend the negative effects of the dominant culture. The negative effects are brought about, for example; by not seeing one's history, culture, or background represented in the textbook or curriculum or by seeing that history, culture, or background distorted. They may result from the staffing pattern in the school when all teachers and principals are white and only the janitor and cafeteria workers are African-American. These non-certified employees are prime examples of tracking of African-American students into the lowest-level classes resulting to low pay wages. The primary aim of culturally relevant teaching is to assist in the development of a "relevant Black personality" that allows African-American students to choose academic excellence yet still identify with Africa and African-American culture.

Brophy (1974) reports that there are teachers who use only one teaching style to teach all students. This involves lower-socioeconomic African-American, Caucasian-American and other minority students who enter inner-city schools at the elementary level with many different learning styles. Bennett (1990) reports that these students have a low rate of retention and a high rate of school failure or early school dropout. Ideally, teachers need to recognize that African-American and Caucasian-American students from lower-socioeconomic backgrounds learn in many different ways.

Jordan Jackson (1999) reminds us that another problem exists. There is a clear picture of how colleges and universities are not fully preparing teachers to teach for academic success among African, Caucasian-American and other minorities students from lower-socioeconomic backgrounds who attend inner-city schools. Hence, the sample chosen for this study shows that students at the elementary levels from inner-city elementary schools are lacking the quality education. These grade levels are crucial to academic success during the child's formative years of learning. It is at these grade levels where students are able to master a considerable amount of knowledge while acquiring a solid foundation of perceptual development conducive to learning. This is why it is imperative that African-American and Caucasian-American students from various middle and upper socioeconomic backgrounds acquire a solid academic background. African, Caucasian-American and other minority students from lower-socioeconomic backgrounds bring into the inner-city classroom distinctive sets of cultural norms and behaviors, which include their history, language, values, rituals, and symbols that are unfamiliar to many white teachers. The development of multiculturalist education and the implicit assumptions that underlie this movement are exemplified by Banks (1986) states not only are African-American students mis-educated, so are Caucasian-American students and many other minorities from rural or back woods areas of the Deep South. The interaction of Afrocentic ideology and educational issues took root with Carter Woodson's (1933) classic book, The Mis-Education Of The Negro. Popularized in the political sphere by Malcolm X, the educational aspects of their learning styles were applied to a wider array of psycho-educational issues in the 1970s, 1980s, and 1990s by such authors as Na'im Arbar, Molefi Kete Asante, Joseph Baldwin, Wade Boykin, Janice Hale-Benson, Barbara Shade, Jawanza Kunjufu, Wade Nobles, Hakim Rashid, and Joseph L. White. In the opinion of these educators and psychologists familiar with Afrocentic philosophical orientations, several traits laid the foundation for what has come to be known as a "learning style" presumably characteristic of African-American students from lower-socioeconomic backgrounds, but Caucasian-American students from the lower-socioeconomic backgrounds were not included in the study because of racism on the part of the poor Caucasian-American adults from lower-socioeconomic backgrounds. Ethnographic research aims to identify these phenomena where there is an incompatibility between teachers, students' preferred learning styles, traditional curriculum, and negative teachers' attitudes (Brown and Louise, 1995). Billings (1990), in her book entitled, <u>The Dream Keeper</u>, supports these findings which arise from culture dissonance.

Mullis (1986) gives a positive view concerning the process of learning with his findings from studying the plight of the African-American child, but dismissed the plight of the Caucasian-American student from lower-socioeconomic backgrounds. The main focus of his theory was to improve academic success among African-American students. Sources on perceptual intelligence, attitude, language, and even neurological tests are the concrete results of the practical work of persons who take them. Having discernible roots in the social world in which they take place, tests such as aptitude and standardized inform us more about the social process in which a subject is engaged than they reveal about the mental capabilities of any subject matter. Standardized tests reflect negative views of lower-socioeconomic African-American and Caucasian-American and other minorities students, but they do not inform us about how teachers present the materials for preparing students to pass tests. Aptitude tests claim to measure intelligence, but these tests are questionable because they measure construct variables that are not absolute and certainly reflect negative views of lower-socioeconomic students (Billings, 1992).

When the issue of class is removed from discussions concerning learning styles, Grant (1992) and Heath (1986) state that all students will excel. Some learning-style theorists argue strenuously that every effort should be made to match instructional methods to the students' identified learning styles (e.g., Dunn & Dunn, 1978). Other theorists adopt a middle-of-the-road approach and argue that African-American and Caucasian-American students should be encouraged to be flexible in their learning styles. Davidman (1991) argues that a matching approach may provide short-term benefits; however, this approach is more likely to stunt the students' intellectual development in the long run. Additionally, other theorists openly acknowledge that some learning styles are detrimental to school success and advocate training for altering student learning styles. In fact, the entire thinking skills movement by Friby (1990) and its application to at-risk

14

students is questionable because more recent educational theories and strategies emphasize the role of socioeconomic background, home environment, and cultural characteristics as determining factors.

Extensive research by Stalling (1990) has delineated many facets and emerging theories on many intelligence and learning styles, including both cognitive and motivational styles for all students from lower socioeconomic background. Stalling states that African-American and Caucasian-American students are experiencing early school failure in inner-city schools.

Initially, researchers such as Billing and Comer (1991) suggest that African-American students whose dominant motivation is failure-oriented are contrasted to other students who are mastery-oriented. Therefore, deprivation theorists, such as Baumeister, Bodsen, and Smart (1985), generally place the fault of failure on African-American students because they are labeled as students of inferiority, but not the Caucasian-American students who are from lower-socioeconomic backgrounds. However, Rich (1994) states inferiority or cultural deprivation does not lie alone within a race. He asserts that failure is caused by selective inattention developed in the politics of everyday life in the classroom.

African-American and Caucasian-American students in exclusive elite schools are instructed in a manner designed to enhance their critical thinking skills. They are taught the value and the process of independent research. They discuss current issues and social problems, giving their opinions readily and often. There is much emphasis on how to present oneself publicly with confidence. However, how to present oneself during classroom activities is still controlled by the teacher. This is why other researchers have taken an interest in the academic success of African-American and Caucasian-American students who are having problems at the elementary levels (Young, 1997). Several strategies for learning have been developed by Slavin and his colleagues at Johns Hopkins University that will enhance the academic stability of many students at risk, such as African-American and Caucasian-American students from lower-socioeconomic backgrounds. These learning programs include: Student Team Achievement Divisions (STAD), Teams-Game-Tournaments (TGT), Team Accelerated Instruction (TAI), and Cooperative Integrated Reading and Composition (CIRC), which are representative of many different cooperative learning styles for academic success. According to Dunn & Dunn (1978), one learning style combined with the child's preferred style of learning does not result in academic success on all occasions.

## CHAPTER IV

## THE IMPACT OF INSTRUCTIONAL STRATEGIES ON THE LEARNING ACHIEVEMENT OF MINORITY STUDENTS FROM LOWER SOCIOECONOMIC BACKGROUNDS

Many teachers understand that all students do not learn by using the same techniques, but at the same time many teachers teach as if all students learn by using only one technique. In the public school system this type of performance by teachers has caused many students to fail, be retained or drop out of school as early as the elementary level. To understand how students learn, teachers should have some knowledge concerning the function of the brain, development of students' modality, and masturation of the students to determine which learning style is appropriate.

The root of the process of learning relating to minority students can be traced back to students' culture. Educators such as: Wright and Wapner (1987) thought schools should provide curricula that meet the needs of every student. He stated, "That a child can not learn if the child's modalities are not fully developed through the stages in its brain." Wright believes that teachers should be a guide for their students during their learning process. This theory based on the process of learning by Wright (1987).

Wapner focused on the masturation of modalities of students during their academic achievement. His theory determines the development of the brain and its readiness for comprehension of learning materials. There are three stages of development that the author refers, they are: reflective, perceptual, and conceptual stages of development. From these stages of learning the author emphasizes the importance of perceptual stage of development, there can not be any comprehension or conceptual development in students until the perceptual stage is developed.

In recent years, minority students who attend elementary school in the United States were considered educationally disadvantaged which has increased Jordan-Jackson, (1987). For example, in 1988, the National Educational Longitudinal Study conducted a study that consisted of elementary minority students from inner city New York. The finding was 41% African-American third graders, 37%, fourth graders, 14% Chicanos, and 8% others ethnic were characterized as having two or more risk factors such as, single parents, siblings who dropped out of school, or home alone after school for three or more hours a day. Furthermore, the Carnegie Council on adolescent development (1998) estimated that about 25% of 10 to 17 year olds extremely vulnerable to multiple high-risk behaviors, such as school failure and substance abuse, and another 25% may be at moderate risk.

MacIver (1990) explore instructional approaches that were limited to minorities, particularly African-American students when it came to choices and problem solving abilities. Educators must teach the explicit rules of the power of culture within the context of school settings and also tap the academic potential of all students.

While developing environments, it is difficult for educators to teach African-American and other minorities with troubling behavior or learning styles. Tasks may present an even greater dilemma for educators who teach African-American students who do not understand the cultural relevance. This apply to any other culture present in the classroom with diversity other than the culture of the teacher. These teachers who are having problems in the classroom teaching African-American and other minorities students must first ask themselves if this is their chosen profession, if they are in the classroom for the sake wanting to be there, or because they want to be a true teacher, think they want to teach, or have the need to teach. If the answer is one of the previous, I suggest you (a) view attitude, and (b) be sensitive to the needs of all students. No educator can really think that he or she knows the affairs of African-American or any other minority student Jordan-Jackson (1999). These educators only understand the forces that affect the researchers' results. Articles in the Journal of Negro Education researched by Lehr (1994) contradict the low-achievers in mathematics. The final result stated that African-American had a negative attitude toward mathematics and the white students did not, could it be that the implementations given in the classroom are the same as those given to African-American students.

With contradictions concerning the articles written by Aiken (1988) and Reyes (1985) which point out factors that describe African-Americans as low achievers, it suggests nothing about the methods presented in the classroom. Research reports that more negative attitudes toward mathematics are among African-African students, and their parents are not concerned with their academic achievement. This is far from the truth. As an educator there is evidence indicating differences in the implementation of instructional strategies used by White teachers when teaching African-American and other minority students from lower socioeconomic backgrounds. For example; Instructional design should be implemented as a vision for teachers to teach mathematics. In many elementary schools in America, many teachers are allowed to teach mathematics without knowing how to implement, encourage, and develop the subject for comprehension by the use of strategies that present a coherent view for students who are minorities. This is why many African-American students from lower socioeconomic backgrounds have a negative attitude toward mathematics in many public schools (Jordan-Jackson, 1999).

The Marcus Garvey Private School—An Afrikan-Center Curriculum, founded in 1975 by Dr. Alvin Palmer, in Los Angeles, California, presents the best example to date of the Afrikan-centered schools, programs, and curricula to boost the intelligence. Academic and social achievement of African American children who are not taught beyond the limits are attained by other alternative educational programs. Afrikan-centered programs base their curricula and pedagogical approaches on the past and contemporary sociohistorical, sociocultural experiences and future goals of Afrikan peoples the world over; on the developmental psychology and characteristics of Afrikan children and adolescents; and on the development in Black students of an operationally stable and enduring Afrikan identity and consciousness.

Award-winning Marcus Garvey School which enrolls children from two years old through ninth-grade, emphasizes academics in its preschool programs. The effectiveness of its Afrikan-center approach can be appreciated by our citation of few of the many remarkable demonstrations by Garvey students which have been noted in many publications.

Two-year-olds learn to recite their alphabet in English, Swahili and Spanish.

Three-year-olds can recite the Latin names of all the major bones in the body and can recognize all fifty states on a map, can name all states and cities their capitals with minimal assistance of their of their teachers.

It is commonplace for four-year-old pre-schoolers to read from third through sixth grade books. In fact, Garvey students are usually three or more grade levels above their national grade average in reading and mathematics.

At Garvey, Algebra is taught in fourth grade and trigonometry and calculus taught in the eighth grade.

Garvey third grade students scored higher on both reading and math than sixth graders from a public school for gifted (predominately White children) on identical tests administered to both classes.

The unusual achievements by Marcus Garvey School are not based an the exclusive admission policy nor on the higher education credentials of its teaching staff. According to Jordan Jackson, (1999) most of the teaching staff does not have a college degree as a matter of school policy. Garvey School success seems to be based on its Afrikan culture perspective. Afrikan-based school culture, its emphasis on providing an Afrikan historical context for all classes and studies, on development of Afrikan identity and consciousness, the development of a positive self-image and pride through the intense study of Afrikan and Afrikan American history individualized attention, and allowing each student to progress at his or her own pace. Moreover, no more than fifteen students are assigned to each teacher, and close parental involvement in maintaining high student motivation and dealing with discipline problems make very significant contributions to the schools success record. Additionally, Culturally-aware teachers hold and express high expectations of their students, and sincerely believe in their students' ability to learn. Teachers are free to initiate, create and innovate in the classroom where the students are taught to deal with real life problems and situations and to believe in themselves.

Whenever there is any success shown among African-American students it's reported as an isolated case, according to Lerher (1994). Whenever educational research demonstrates some degree of success, it has been at isolated schools or in rare sub districts that have had moderate success in increasing the achievement levels. One can assume if there is a positive attitude with these students, even through there is a continuous struggle with achievement gaps between White students from middle and upper class, African-American and other minority students have a right to a quality education. Cambridge, Ma and Montclair, NJ are cited examples of the latter Carnegie Foundation for the Advancement of Teaching. However, no large urban school system has been able to spread the success of individual programs. For example; the Detroit Public Schools have adopted the goal of becoming the first urban district to successfully educate their students as their mission.

The family circumstances of youth living in inner cities are also alarming. Approximately 20% of the youth living in America live below the poverty level and the largest concentration of poor students are in urban schools. Frelberg 1991, believes the number of students and youth living in poverty is expected to more than double by the year 2206, students from poor families are three times more likely to become dropouts than students from economically advantaged homes. These findings and other indicators like the high levels of crime, unemployment, drug dependency, broken families, illegitimacy rates, density of liquor stores, and concentrated poverty, clearly describe the critical status of students who are currently living in our nation's inner-cities. They represent the most imperiled group of our increasing number of students at the verge of falling (Pedra, 1991).

# CHAPTER V

# THE APPROPRIATE STRATEGIES USED IN THE CLASS FOR ACADEMIC SUCCESS AMONG STUDENTS FROM LOWER SOCIOECONOMIC BACKGROUNDS

Teaching is a means to an end; responses are effective only when it leads to value and change in students. The desire to become a skilled and effective teacher must begin by using the knowledge brought in the classroom by each student which is culture relevance. This is where many students learn effectively from their innateness. Eliminating theory is the first step of effective teaching. With this elimination, students from lower socioeconomic backgrounds are allowed openness for cultural relevance.

According to Billings' "Cultural Relevance" moves beyond language to include other aspects for students from lower socioeconomic backgrounds and school culture. White teachers who only teach from the aspects of their culture do so as if their culture is the only culture transcend results with negative effects. These negative effects are brought about, for example, by not understanding the history of students, especially African-American students from lower socioeconomic backgrounds. This history has been distorted in the minds of many white teachers and moved on to the textbooks and learning materials in schools curricula and having perceived notions that African-American students can not learn because of the color of their skin. The primary aim of culturally relevant teaching is to assist in the development of a "relevant personality which allows all students from lower socioeconomic backgrounds to choose academic excellence which facilitates self identity with all cultures in the school system. With the teaching of cultural relevance teachers will pay close attention to African-African students perception first, rather than their conception development. Those who teach African-American students and other students from lower socioeconomic backgrounds must realize the sporadic learning styles. For example, study was conducted by the author in the Southern portion of the United States with students attending elementary grade schools. My study using an interview tool was found to be in the interest of several schools in the Mid-West.

An example of cultural relevance was an appropriate profile where I briefly interviewed a group of teachers for the study. It was a small ethnographic study that included only eight teachers, but only six responded. Unlike most traditional studies, my study did not call for objective measures to identify teachers' proficiency. They were interviewed for their insights into good teaching. In essence, I asked them during the interview to identify their educational stands that they felt were important to enhance Blacks, and other minorities students academic development. Five Black teachers and three white teachers were included in the study. All women, ranged in experience from eight to thirty years of teaching experience. They had taught in a variety of schools including rural White and Integrated schools of the suburban and of the poorest of the inner-city. One had attended an Historically Black College and the others predominately white state institutions.

The interview questions concerned "Culture Relevance." This term refers, according to Gloria Ladson, to the cultural group (including ethnic and racial characteristics) that teachers most closely identify. The author was well aware that many White teachers had no clue what the term Cultural Relevance meant, as well as a few African-American teachers because of their educational background. The author selected examples believed most illustrative of each aspect.

My experience with White teachers, both preservice and novice, indicate that many are uncomfortable and some are afraid of student differences, particularly racial differences. Some teachers made such statements as "I don't really see color, I just see children", These are some and the same remarks made by teachers interviewed by Gloria Billings stated, "I don't care if they are, red, green, or polka dot, I just treat them all like children." There is a mask which is described as "dysconscious racism" an "uncertified habit of mind that justifies inequality and exploitation by accepting the existing order of things as green" (Billings.1989).

One dimension of culturally relevant teaching is the teachers' perceptions of themselves and others. Too often teachers have a poor opinion of themselves and their profession by thinking and exhibiting the point that they are interested in the education of all children. In contrast, teachers who practice culturally relevant methods not only see themselves as professionals, but also strongly identify with teaching.

I began my individual profiles of teachers' interviews of my study with whom exemplifies these qualities.

Angelica Smith is a graduate from Indiana State university with a degree in Elementary Education, and has been a pre-kindergarten teacher for thirty-six years. She is a Black teacher who believes that Black students have the ability to accomplish academically at all costs; but are not given the opportunity in many cases to do so by school administrators, teachers and staff. She believes that if bureaucracy would remove itself from education it would be better for all concerned.

Teachers with culturally relevant practices see themselves as part of the community, see teaching as giving back to their community, and encourage their students to do the same. This quality is very evident in Mrs. Smith's work as a wife, mother, and teacher. She has lived in the community most of her teaching career. She attended Indians State University and graduated with qualified credentials, but taught as a substitute teachers for six years before being hired as a full-time teacher. She is presently employed as a teacher in the same school district.

Mrs. Smith's classroom described as one of "organized chaos" It is a busy classroom resided over by a busy teacher. Mrs. Smith constantly looks for materials and supplies to purchase for her students. She takes advantage of special offers and bargains for classroom teachers by publishers and teacher supply stores. I taught Mrs. Smith's class on several occasions before meeting her." Mrs. Smith's classroom was far advanced than any other classroom. Secondly, I interviewed Odell Cook, a graduate from Fisk University with a degree in chemistry, and Bradley University with a degree in Elementary Education. Mrs. Cook felt that many Black students suffered from what she described as a "cultural deficits." She is a fourth grade teacher who believed in teaching current evidents, history of famous African-Americans who were discounted as achievers by White America, and having her students to read many books on ancient African History. I don't think Mrs. Cook has seen the top of her desk in years. She spends so much of her time at her students' desks giving one-on-one assistance. Mrs. Cook had the opportunity to teach school in a more affluent elementary school, but she prefers to stay and teach Black students as well as live in the same community. During the interview she gave me personal reasons why. "As a little girl, I always had the desire to become a teacher. After acquiring my second college degree I was hired as a substitute teacher which paid very little, but carrying a full-time load I remained focus on teaching Black students. She commented that she always told her students that a good education was worth its weight in gold and that their community needs them.

Mrs. Reid was also interviewed. She taught fifth grade, a graduated from a Historically Black College where she was trained as a teacher and an anthropologist. She believes in cooperative learning which she feels is relevant to her methods and style of teaching. She believes techniques associated with cooperative learning motivates her students when being implemented in her classroom. For example, rather than allow her students to rely on the traditional romantic story of some famous persons allowed to work together on one story as a group. Mrs. Reid provides her students with more accurate pictures: "Now, I know your book talks about Nat Turner, but it doesn't give you the whole story… You have never seen nor have you ever read anything positive about him. Nat Turner was a minister in North Carolina during slavery. He was also an activist. Turner did not wait for anything to happen he made things happen. He did a good job and you as students should work in your community and whatever you do, Do it well."

Another well rounded teacher who was interviewed, Dora Brown. Mrs. Brown bonds with her students by sitting in a seat beside her students, and giving them individualized help. Having the students to talk to her after she explains a difficult task that will assure he or she that they understand the perception. She has students talk to her after she explains a difficult task, to ensure that they understand the assignment. Students begin to explain the process to Mrs. Brown. Throughout the explanation Mrs. Brown makes sure that the perception of the subject is clear before moving on.

Miss Elizabeth James defines her relationship with her students as an extended family. When she was born her mother died four days later leaving her a ward of the state. She is flexible about specific classroom expectations. She also and helps students formulate expectations they can meet and survive within any situation in life by teaching life skills. My last interview was the only White teacher, Mrs. McCall decided to become a teacher when she entered junior high school. She never wanted to do anything else. She believes that all students can learn and that they really do want to learn, although they don't always know appropriate ways to behave in school or to facilitate their knowledge. Her belief is that children have more ways of learning than teachers know how to teach, and teachers need to listen as well as talk with students. Her assumption is that schools should be morally obligated to do everything possible to make sure that all students acquire the basic tools of learning the most fundamental being reading. She thinks it is important to teach all students how to learn facts rather than memorize facts. She thinks students should be encouraged to study. For example, she states, "I do not often spell words for my first graders, instead, I urge them to say the word slowly and write down the sound they hear themselves. I also try to help students see connection between knowing the new information and using their skills in each area all day long." For instance, in math we use literature and link it in all areas of subject matters discuss serious difficulties in behaviors that are found in everyday life. She believes that there should be less theory and more hands-on when teaching these students.

From the interviews and teachers' participation there was much information that could have been gathered, but because of the limited time, not only for teachers, but students as well. Further study was conducted in march of "99" by the author. The findings are presented in the latter portion of the book.

A final note about the teachers. Five of the eight teachers were Black; the remaining three were White, but only one of them responded to the interview.

Those that were interviewed saw that state, federal and local government neglected the education of Black students by not allocating funds assist in their education. In these neglected areas of the inner-cities teachers taught and wanted to work in order to help. Each was offered the opportunity to teach in other areas less stressful. But, all of them remained in order teacher those whom are neglected by giving them a change to learn and develop academically this means, when African-American students and other students are taught cultural relevance it motivate students to learn through perception.

Perceptual development give students the understanding of why and how to motive their where and what is the great contribution Wampan's hypothetical models of perceptual modalities.

If teachers use appropriate strategies, low-achieving students from lower-socioeconomic backgrounds can perform with the same frequency of participation as other students classified as middle- and upper-socioeconomic backgrounds (Amidon & Simon, 1965).

In general, research on teachers' expectations is clear. The images that teachers and other educators have about African-American and Caucasian-American students from lower-socioeconomic backgrounds at the elementary level in inner-city schools have major influences on student success. For example, if teachers believe that a student's intellect is low, teachers will adjust their teaching levels (Chun, 1987-88). Research by Hamilton and Gingress (1993) indicated that teachers who interact positively with African-American and Caucasian students from middle- and upper-class situations do so by challenging them intellectually, calling upon them and praising them often in the class.

Ogbus (1992) reported that African-American and Caucasian-American students from lower-socioeconomic backgrounds, even though they have made some gain in academic performance, continue to lag behind their African-American and Caucasian-American from middle- and upper-class cohort groups. He believed that this lag is a result from the fact a significant number of African-American and Caucasian-American parents from the lower-socioeconomic backgrounds did not attain a shared sense of societal values, skills, and knowledge which can foster competence in their children.

If a teacher uses appropriate strategies, all minorities students from lower socioeconomic backgrounds can perform on the same level or abstraction and with the frequency of participation as other students classified as-middle- and upper-socioeconomic backgrounds (Amidon &Simon, 1965).

In general, research on teachers' expectation is clear. The images that teachers and other educators have about African-American and Caucasian-American from lower-socioeconomic backgrounds at the elementary level in inner-city schools have major influences on students success. For example, if teachers believe that student's intellect is low, teachers will adjust their teaching levels (Chun, 1987-88). Researchers Hamilton and Gingriss (1993)indicated that teachers interact with African-American and Caucasian students from middle and upper-class situations do so by challenging them intellectually calling upon them and praising them often in the class and intellectually challenge white, male, middle and upper class students more often whereas they reprimand African-

American males and students from lower socioeconomic backgrounds. However, teachers asked less questions of student who are minorities from lower socioeconomic backgrounds and considered them as low achievers. These students are usually given the easiest questions.

Teachers were less likely to provide clues or to rephrase the questions for these students for their answers. Consequently, the teachers' questioning may be less helpful or encouraging What is the impact of a hidden curriculum relating to Students from lower socioeconomic backgrounds.

# CHAPTER VI

# HIDDEN CURRICULUM/TRACKING FOR FAILURE

A hidden curriculum, teaches the majority of African-American students and other students from lower socioeconomic backgrounds obedience and deference to authority, docility, subordination, extrinsic motivation, external control, dependence, and fatalism. The results from such behaviors will ultimately stagnate African-American students to lower paying employment with low self-concept and the feeling of inferiority.

An instrument of interviews was used by Anyon and Rist which provided illuminating examples of just how a hidden curriculum operates in two different sites, one in a lower socioeconomic arena and the other in an elite setting.

Anyon (1981) interviewed teachers and principals in four schools in one school district. All the classes were fifth grades. What she discovered was that although the curriculum objectives were the same for all these students, the hidden curriculum provided drastically different experiences for students from lower socioeconomic backgrounds.

The students in the elite school were instructed in a manner designed to enhance their critical thinking skills. They were taught the value and the processes of an independent research, they discussed current issues and social problems, and they were encouraged to give their opinions readily without grade attack. There was much emphasis on how to present oneself publicly and confidently. Teachers accomplished this goal in a number of ways, including elimination of bells that demarcated time and obedient behavior, of controlling the movement of the class. The teachers were never nasty or impolite, nor did they shout direct orders to these students. The level of these students confidence was high and they knew they were destined to be the owners and controllers of large corporations with means of production. But, on the other hand, in schools that were not the elite, teachers attempted to control the movement of their classes through negotiations in which the students were constantly probed to evaluate the consequence of their misbehavior. Anyone states that these students were acquiring the symbolic or cultural capital that would prepare them for managerial and professional careers. Symbolic capital includes a strong commitment to hard work and the work ethic, an internal locus of control, and firm belief in the value of competition.

Hidden curriculum also reinforce-American students, particularly from lower-socioeconomic backgrounds as incapable and inferior. In a study conducted by Jackson, (2000) found that it was decided that students as early as pre-k could not learn, they were virtually written off as failures at the age of three. In spite of student effort, performance, and ability, the teachers in Jackson's study ignore data that disconfirmed their stereotypes and prejudices. This study illustrate how schools often collaborate in the environment where adversity range with inequality, and the unequal status of African-American students who are poor.

Tracking is a far cry from the vision of Horace Mann. Today the use of tracking is widespread and continues to separate children by race and class, resulting in the maintenance and reproduction of a system of social and economic stratification. It starts early in the lives of school children. A study conducted by Rist, (1970) indicated that teachers who made permanent placement assignments by the eighth day of kindergarten is starting the tracking process groups, high, average, or low. Students are categorized like animals with academic expectation concerning students' achievement, behavior, future success, and home life. Students are also track to produce various diplomas such as vocational, general, academic, or advanced academic. The number of certificates of attendance, statements basically verifying that students' attended school but failed to achieve is growing. In many states a general diploma given in some school districts in Illinois and the state of Georgia for instance, do not prepare students to be unconditionally admitted to any of its public four-year state schools. In addition, tracking is an administrative convenience. Students have to be partitioned into smaller instructional groups, and dividing them by ability, on the surface, seems to be sound educational practice. Defenders of the education system claim that it allows for individualized instruction, the development of more positive student self-concepts, and more effective and efficient instruction. But there is overwhelming research evidence that tracking students by ability has no educational benefit for students and in fact is deleterious to academic achievement, extracurricular participation, self-concept, peer relationship, career aspirations and motivation. Many works support the conclusion that the practice of tracking is indeed curious as little evident supports its use in school (Goodlad, 1984; Gouldner, 1978; Hallinan & Sorensen, 1983; Research generated by Oakes (1954) and others supports Benjamin Bloom's assertion that placement in a low academic track has a devastating impact on a student's self-esteem. Worse yet, because there are real differences in the content of what is being taught, academic tracking may, in fact, contribute even more to academic failure.

How a student gets into a particular track depends on a number of factors. Gilmore (1985) concluded that teachers' perception of black students' attitude was a more important factor than their academic ability for placement, in high-track classes. Findley and Bryan (1975), on the other hand, found that 83% of school districts nationwide used achievement or IQ tests for placement. The tests provide the guise of objectivity and accountability used to defend the placements. The mere proliferation of these instruments and the profit-making business that administer them are also related to the extensive use of standardized tests in educational decision making.

The mere finding that schools assign to different curricula does not necessarily indicate educational malpractice, nor is the assignment entirely unjustified. Students vary in ability, motivation, persistence, learning style, and numerous other personality traits and behaviors. What is devastating about tracking is that in lower track the number of students from lower socioeconomic back grounds both African-American students who are disproportionately placed in special education classes; where the instructions are inferior and ineffective. Caucasian-American and other minorities that fit these same economic and emotional status are prime target students as well.

When tracking is combined with student characteristics of race and class, the result is predictable. African-American and other poor students are disproportionately tracked by teachers and administrators.

African-American and Caucasian-American students from lower-socioeconomic backgrounds who attend inner-city schools are almost never exposed to what educators call a high-status knowledge, especially at the elementary level in the inner-cities. This information may be useful for the preparation of future teachers from our colleges and universities. According to Dehyle (1986), current pedagogical practice is based upon instruction that does not effectively and actively engage the students' background knowledge and concepts that are targeted during instructions. Pedagogically induced learning problems may arise when there is little congruence between current teaching approaches and the unique learning characteristics that African-American and Caucasian-American students from lower-socioeconomic backgrounds bring to the learning environment.

Such learning characteristics may include motivational styles, cognitive style, social organizational, and sociolinguistic factors. In addition, other factors may be involved, such as differing participant structures, unique question styles, physical features of the classroom, and the lack of instructional materials. Teaching methods and strategies teachers use in the classrooms can be reinforced through a student's strongest modalities. It is frequently assumed that African-American and Caucasian-American students from lower-socioeconomic backgrounds, at the levels of 3rd and 6th grades, fail to learn in the current instructional environment because of an inherent deficiency rather than from a set of external conditions or curriculum which may significantly affect the level of academic performance (Bloom, 1954). It is essential for educators to understand the meaning of modality when it comes to teaching African-Americans from lower-socioeconomic backgrounds, to be able to determine a students's specific strengths and weaknesses and understand how constraints can affect a student's ability to learn (Wright, 1987).

Jackson, (1999) summarized the behavior of teachers who teach lower-track students, and the instructional methods that contribute to the further decline of these struggling, low-achieving students; but the author adds, not only do this list apply to African-American students, but also apply to other minority students from lower socioeconomic backgrounds.

1.  Teachers do not give time for lowers to answer.
2.  Teachers give lowers the answer or call on someone else rather than trying to improve lowers' responses by giving clues or repeating or rephrasing the question.
3.  Teachers ignore incorrect answers by lower's without giving any assistance to guide lowers toward correct answers.
4.  Teachers criticize lowers more often for failure.
5.  Teachers pay less attention to lowers than highs for success.
6.  Teachers fail to give feedback to the public responses of lowers.
7.  Teachers pay less attention to lowers or interact with them with less frequency.
8.  Teachers call on lowers farther away from themselves.
9.  Teachers seat lowers farther away from themselves.
10. Teachers demand less from lowers by teaching them less, by giving less extended explanations and definitions, and by accepting poor quality and often inaccurate responses.
11. Teachers interact with lowers more publicly than privately teachers grade lowers more harshly.
12. Teachers are less friendly to lowers, smiling less often in interactions of lowers.
13. Teachers provide less direct instructions to lowers, giving them less opportunities to practice independently (Jackson, 1997).
14. Teachers provide less meaningful discussion of stories for lowers.
15. Teachers allow lowers to read silently without guidance as to comprehension (Jackson, 1999).

African-American and other students from lower socioeconomic backgrounds are constantly faced with situations in their environment that require critical thinking skills. Many inner-city schools are threatening environments where survival depends on critical reasoning which enables these students to solve problems, analyze, ask relevant questions, and observe astutely for positive results. This is essential even for minority students who do not live in America's inner-cities. They need instruction in critical thinking skills in order to respond to overt and subtle racist behaviors that they are likely to encounter. African-American students' physical and emotional well-being depends on the ability to judge credible sources, look for alternatives and evidence, detect bias, distinguish between facts and opinions, understand contradictions of words and behaviors, and analyze the unstated as well as the stated.

Finally, tracking affects students' self-concepts, their relationships with peers teachers and their career aspiration. The results of tracking cause students to feel alienated, feel inferior, excluded, and negative about themselves. Their interactions with their peers were confrontational and accompanied by frequent outbursts of yelling, swearing, talking of one's mother and fighting. The relationship between teachers and students are negative for lower-track students. Lower-track students think that teaches are punitive as well as lack concern for them (Jordan Jackson, 1999).

What makes the tracking system so pernicious is that once students are assigned to a track, students seldom move either up or down. Jordan Jackson (1999) compares the tracking system to a form of gladiator during the Biblical time: "When you win, you move only the right to go to the next round until you graduate and become independent in society." The author found that tracking is a down hill battle with no outlet. When students are labeled as low-achievers they are affixed at the elementary level. A paper trail is created which follow these students throughout high school which becomes a self-fulfilling prophecy for them. These inflexible and unyielding placement assume that one's intelligence is measurable, unidimensional, fixed, and unalterable and that achievement is general, not special to subject.

African-American students are particularly injured by this practice because their race and class are associated with low achievement. Once placed in the lower tracks, students are taught less effectively, they interact hastily with teachers and peers, and they developed negative self-esteem. All of these results lead to a vicious cycle of school failure and antisocial behaviors. However, African-American and other minority students must learn to take responsibility for their behaviors and attitudes that lead to non-achievement, but the educational profession must bear the responsibility for its failure to provide an equal educational opportunity.

# CHAPTER VII

# INSTRUCTIONAL STRATEGIES/TEACHER EXPECTATIONS DOES RACE MATTER

Just as deaf and blind children learn how to read by the use of their strongest modalities, all children need to be taught by the use of the same strategies, especially students from lower-socioeconomic backgrounds. These students are not only denied implementation of their strongest modality in the classrooms, but are also forced to participate in unfamiliar learning styles (Bennett, 1986). Children who are able to see and hear are fortunate because they can use their hearing and vision to learn to read. There are other students who do not learn well through their modalities. They may use senses other than sight and vision that are comparatively stronger, making it easier for them to learn and remember (e.g., associating words with objects or numbers with names). Therefore, it seems that instructional strategies and methods and strengths and weaknesses of modalities that will enhance the teaching all students may not fully be considered by many educators.

Erickson (1986) stated that learning is the gateway to success. For students from lower-socioeconomic backgrounds, there are obvious differences between what educators consider standard English and how students from lower-socioeconomic backgrounds speak, enunciate their words, use vocabulary, use rhythm in their speech, and how they pace themselves and reflect upon their performance. There are assumptions regarding what is spoken and left unspoken, whether one interrupts or defers to others, and whether one asks direct or indirect questions.

Lesniak, Lohman and Curukian (1972) compared verbal behaviors between inner-city schools and found that the inner-city teachers gave more directions, criticized their students more, asked fewer questions, and accepted or clarified students ideas less. whereas, African-American teachers, according to Coleman (1966), found differences between the learning approaches of high- and low-achieving African-American and Caucasian-American students from lower-socioeconomic backgrounds when it came to academic success. African-American and Caucasian-American students who were high achievers were motivated and preferred less structure than low achievers. Beachman (1994) found that African-American students who were high achievers shared similar learning styles with middle- and upper-class Caucasian-American students. These findings are consistent with Boutte (1990).

Society can determine if teachers consider race when teaching students of diversity. Teachers will often make remarks as if they are not conscious of race

31

awareness when teaching. Therefore, teachers who implement this type of conduct should not be in the teaching profession because race does matter.

## INSTRUCTIONAL TASKS REASONS FOR SCHOOL FAILURE

Bloom's (1954) study stated that methods and strategies teachers use that contribute to the failure of students from lower-socioeconomic backgrounds were being taught from simple watered-down curricula. These curricula, according to Bloom (1954), were designed for failure. They consisted of fewer opportunities for students with no motivational aspects. African-American and Caucasian-American students from lower-socioeconomic backgrounds were not taught to answer higher-level questions because school administrators, teachers, and staff thought of those students as a menace to society and determined their fate by labeling them as low achievers Cooper (1979). Good and Brophy (1972), O'Leary and Grant (1977) studied teachers' reasons for giving praise in the classroom. Low achievers received few teacher interactions in three categories.

Beacham (1990) suggested that low achievement was directly related to teachers' criticism and lack of praise for learning performance. With respect to "the methods" of teaching, some authors suggest that African-American and Caucasian-American students from lower-socioeconomic backgrounds have a low tolerance for boredom relative to African-American and Caucasian-American students from middle- and upper-class (Boykin, 1984). Therefore, lessons must include high levels of motor activity, stimulation, and vivacity in order for African-American and Caucasian students from lower-socioeconomic grounds to be motivated to achieve (Boykin, 1978 and Holt, 1964).

Hooks (1990) suggested that teachers need to exhibit warmth and incorporate verbal interplay during instruction, with a rhythmic style of speech and distinctive intonation in their speech patterns, in order to build good rapport with African-American and Caucasian-American students. Billings (1978) argued that African-American and Caucasian-American students from lower-socioeconomic backgrounds need intense group-oriented and interpersonal learning. Smith (1986) argued that in order to meet the educational needs of African-American and Caucasian-American students teachers need to incorporate visual, kinesthetic, and tactile teaching strategies, role-playing and sociodramatic teaching strategies, individualized contacts, computer-assisted instruction, and one-on-one tutoring.

Hale (1986) asserted that there is a culture-based difference in how African-American and Caucasian-American students from lower-socioeconomic backgrounds communicate and process information. Unfortunately, educators tend to treat the stylistic mismatch between some students and schools as a student deficiency and as a problem that requires students to change. As a result, educators fail to see potential for enriching school experience for all children. Moreover, they fail to see that the traditional school style has severe limitations. However, when it comes to teaching African-American and Caucasian students from lower-socioeconomic backgrounds, there are limitations. Educators tend to misinterpret historical backgrounds of many different cultures, including learning styles, customs, values, morals, and rituals that lie within the many subcultures of African-American and Caucasian-American students from lower-socioeconomic backgrounds. One wonders why there is so much school failure among students from lower socioeconomic backgrounds.

Let's borrow a business analogy, students are the consumer, the product is a workable curriculum presented by administrators and teachers, whose focus is to present this workable curriculum with returns and profits. The business product, is the "curriculum," determines student performance.

The quality and quantity of the teachers' input was fixed; they supplied the curriculum. The teachers then treated that curriculum with their ability to implement and affect students' perception; the end product is great returns from students which result variation in performance merely illustrate different levels of effort and abilities among students at all levels. But in the business of education, many different types of products (materials of curriculum) are distributed without check and balance just as it is in the political arena. The educational system need the same type of protection to protect students academic achievements.

In thirty years little has changed concerning the education of minority youth at the elementary level. The average achievement of many of these students is below what is expected. This means that the social class is becoming as powerful for Caucasian-American students from lower socioeconomic backgrounds as it for African-American and other minorities students when it comes to predicting the academic performance. Therefore, the average performance of all students, marginalis and mainstream alike has apparently declined. Although a variety of explanations and remedies have been offered to vindicate or improve the issue of school and quality remains salient. Many negative reports have been given concerning education after the decision of Brown vs, the Board of Education; such as; minorities from lower socioeconomic backgrounds who attend schools in neighborhoods of the elite are considered inferior in quality of instruction and resources.

As a student growing up in the state of Mississippi, during my elementary and high school years, on many occasions as an African-American student from a lower socioeconomic backgrounds, I received used textbooks from schools of the so called white elite students. Now, just think about it, one could say if I used textbooks that were handed down to the lower socioeconomic backgrounds me and others students in the South, one should come the conclusion that students of the elite were also given an inferior education which resulted in academic failure. One might ask the question, what is an inferior education? Is society speaking of materials in the schools or the facilities that are inferior. I think this is a fair question to ask. If I and other African-American students received the elite white students' materials after they finished them or received new ones, didn't we all receive an inferior education, both elite and poor, or does this mean only African-American students can receive an inferior education because of the status and the color of the skin?

Anelauskas confirms that America's public education at the elementary level ranks below every industrial competitor it has in the world. Poor showing of American students relative to those from other counties was highlighted quite a while ago in the oft-cited 1983 report on the state of American students were never first or second and, in comparison with other industrialized nations were last seven times." The report warned that this threatens our very future as a nation and a people." It pointed out that "international" comparisons of student achievement reveal that on nineteen academic tests American students were never first or second and in comparison with other industrialized nations were last seven times." Anelauskas continues to report concerning the truth about America's educational foundations of our society which are being eroded by a rising tide of mediocrity that threatens our very future as a nation and people. The situation is no better today than at the time when <u>A Nation at Risk</u> was published. In many respects it is much worse, because the gap between American educational achievement and achievement in other countries has widened since 1983, and is growing wider with each passing year." According to former Secretary of Labor Will Brock, public education at the elementary level ranks below every industrial competitor in the world."

There are many factors in the educational system at the elementary level, in grades three and six, that cause African-American and Caucasian-American students to fail or to be successful. These factors lie in the ramification of instructional strategies used by teachers in the classrooms, behavioral attitudes that teachers have toward African-American and Caucasian-American students from lower-socioeconomic backgrounds, teachers' expectations, school curriculum, learning styles African-American and Caucasian-American students bring into the classroom that are ignored by teachers, and the lack of knowledge of African-American culture and the culture of Caucasian-American students from lower-socioeconomic backgrounds by many Caucasian-American teachers (Billings, 1994). Therefore, major changes are needed regarding these factors to promote success for African-American and Caucasian-American students from lower-socioeconomic backgrounds at the elementary level.

Today, teachers are expected to acquire the knowledge that will improve the academic performance of all students, especially for African-American and Caucasian-American students from lower-socioeconomic backgrounds who attend schools in the inner-cities.

## CHAPTER VIII

## RESEARCH ON TEACHER-STUDENT INTERACTIONS: EFFECTS OF STUDENT RACE, GENDER, AND GRADE LEVEL

### Pilot Study

In a pilot study conducted by Jordan, (1998) students from five elementary schools were randomly surveyed with students from socioeconomic backgrounds and their teachers in the inner-city schools. Interviews concerning the types of behaviors/expectations, instructional strategies, tasks, activities, school curriculum, and learning outcomes they use in their classrooms.

The limitations of previous teacher instructional strategies research were addressed in a study (Jordan, 1998) conducted by this author. The study examined (a) quantity and quality of teachers' concerning their implementation of school curriculum at the elementary level; (b) students' perception of teachers' from school curriculum for academic success; (c) the extent to which teachers' implement and students' perception representative of school curricula at the elementary level; and (d) the extent to which teachers implement instructional strategies for academic success for students from lower socioeconomic backgrounds. These issues were discussed in relation to student's race, gender, grade level and location.

Interviews were used to collect data concerning the success and failure of Students from lower socioeconomic backgrounds from elementary grade levels; third and sixth (Jordan, 1998). This study was conducted in five elementary schools in the Mid-western states.

Results from the pilot study indicated that students at the elementary level were fully aware that curricula used in their schools were not preparing them for future endeavors. Teacher behaviors and expectations were rated very low when it came to classroom activities for students from lower-socioeconomic backgrounds. The pilot findings also indicated that teachers were not sensitive to students' academic needs and, on many occasions, students expressed their feelings toward their teachers in many negative ways.

The information required a measurement of the teachers' implementation of school curricula for students at the elementary levels from lower-socioeconomic backgrounds. A T-test was computed, together with a descriptive unit analysis of questionnaire items and interviews. Inferential conclusions include comparisons of teachers' implementation of materials and students' academic success or failure. Means and standard deviations from feedback categories were computed for each item for teachers and students. A content analysis was performed relative to the questionnaires and interviews (Waxman, Wang, Linvall, & Anderson, 1988). Other information required a measurement of the students' perceptions of their teachers' implementing materials in the classroom for students from lower-socioeconomic backgrounds for academic success or failure. A T-test was computed together with a descriptive unit analysis of questionnaires and interviews. Inferential conclusions include comparison of teachers' implementation of materials from the schools' curricula and students' perceptions of the curricula for academic success or failure. Means and standard deviation tables for feedback categories computed for each item for students and teachers. A content analysis was performed relative to the questionnaires and interviews. More important information required a measurement of teachers' instructional strategies implemented in the classroom and the comprehension of these instructional strategies by students at third- and sixth-grade levels from lower-socioeconomic backgrounds. A T-test was performed, plus a descriptive and inferential analysis, in order to compare the differences between the means of instructional strategies and students' comprehension of these instructional strategies academic failure or academic success where means and standard deviation tables were computed for each item for teachers and students. A content analysis was performed relative to the questionnaires and interviews. Finally, a one-way analysis of variance test (ANOVA) test was computed for comparison of the schools in the Midwest and Southern portion of the United States.

# CHAPTER IX

# TABLES/FINDINGS/QUANTITATIVE AND QUALITIES

## Table 1

### Demographic Characteristics of Total Sample

| Characteristic | Levels | Frequency | % |
|---|---|---|---|
| Gender | Male | 236 | 51.6 |
|  | Female | 221 | 48.4 |
| Race | Black | 361 | 79 |
|  | White | 96 | 21 |
| Grade | Third | 241 | 52.7 |
|  | Sixth | 216 | 47.3 |
| Location | MS BWC | 59 | 12.9 |
|  | MS GW | 56 | 12.3 |
|  | MS LH | 61 | 13.3 |
|  | MSLW | 43 | 9.4 |
|  | MSRW | 57 | 12.5 |
|  | MSCH | 49 | 10.5 |
|  | IL CC | 132 | 28.9 |
| STATES | MS | 325 | 71.1 |
|  | IL | 132 | 28.9 |

Note: N = 457.

The results of Table 1 indicate the total sample of the research participants by states and schools.

Two surveys were administered in this study. A 19-item questionnaire measuring student perceptions of the teacher implementation was completed by 436 students. A 19-item questionnaire measuring teacher perceptions of curriculum implementation was completed by 15 teachers and 6 administrators. The items on student and teacher surveys were not identical but, in some instances, could be paired to determine differences in perceptions of curriculum implementation. Items on both surveys measured behavior exhibited by teachers in the classroom, student behavior, teacher interaction, and instructional strategies pertinent to implementing school curricula for third and sixth grades. The two instruments used in the study were examined by a panel of professors in the Department of Curriculum and Instruction to determine both validity and reliability.

## Research Question 1

Research Question 1 states: In what ways do teachers implement school curricula for their third- and sixth-grade classrooms?

The participants responded to a Likert scale:

(1) = strongly disagree,
(2) = disagree,
(3) = neutral,
(4) = agree, and
(5) = strongly agree.

## Quantitative

A frequency test was run to indicate ways teachers implemented the school curriculum for their third- and sixth-grade classrooms. The teacher survey showed that of teachers who taught at the third-and sixth-grade levels 12.3% of the teachers agree and 85.7% strongly agree that they encourage study in the classroom for their third- and sixth-grade students. See Table 2 and Table 3.

## Table 2
## Third-Grade Teachers

| Valid | Frequency | % |
|-------|-----------|-----|
| Strongly agree | 7 | 85.7 |
| Agree | 1 | 14.3 |
| | | |
| Strongly agree | 7 | 85.7 |
| Agree | 1 | 14.7 |
| | | |
| Strongly agree | 7 | 85.7 |
| Agree | 1 | 14.7 |

Note: N = 8

The only reported frequencies and percentages were strongly agree and agree which were the highest and lowest indicated in the research for third-grade students.

The results indicated that teachers (see Tables 4 and 5) felt they were doing everything possible for students' academic success even though their students were from lower-socioeconomic backgrounds.

## Table 3

## <u>Sixth-Grade Teachers</u>

| Valid | Frequency | % |
|---|---|---|
| Strongly agree | 6 | 87.7 |
| Agree | 1 | 12.3 |
| | | |
| Strongly agree | 6 | 85.7 |
| Agree | 1 | 12.3 |

<u>Note</u>: N = 7

Overall, 19 participants responded on the Likert scale with a range from 1-5. All percentages indicated strongly agree and agree for all 19 items on the survey questionnaire.

Additionally, the means for teachers' responses for all 19 items from the teacher survey ranged from agree to strongly agree. The means for the highest items from the teacher survey were 2, 3, 4, 8, 10, 11, 12, 13, 14, 16, 17, and 19. The highest mean was 5.00, second highest was 4.71, with item 1 as third highest, and the lowest items 9, 7, 6, respectively.

## Table 4

## T-Tests for Third- and Sixth-Grade Teachers

| Item | Grade Level | | Df | T | P |
|------|-------------|---|----|----|----|
| | $3^{rd}$ | $6^{th}$ | | | |
| 8 | 5.00 | 3.86 | 15 | 2.18 | .04 |
| 10 | 5.00 | 4.63 | 15 | 2.18 | .05 |
| 15 | 5.00 | 4.63 | 15 | 2.18 | .05 |

Note. N = 9 for $3^{rd}$ grade and N = 8 for $6^{th}$ grade

This table contains means, t scores, and other valves regarding grade levels and teachers. Only the statistics for variables with significant t-values *p (two-tailed tests) <.05 were reported.

A T-test was performed in order to determine the differences between third and sixth grade teachers' perceptions. The results of the tests revealed that significant differences existed for items 8,10, and 15. While the third grade teachers reported means of 5.00 for the three items, the means for sixth grade teachers were considerably lower for item 8 (3.86), item 10 (3.88), and item 15 (4.63).

## Qualitative

Teachers who teach at third- and sixth-grade levels have many different ways to implement their school curricula that they expressed during their interviews. Some teachers stated during their interviews.

They used hidden curricula for academic success. The results were consistent with Good & Brophy (1971) and Keneal (1991) who reported that when students are perceived as failures at the elementary level, experiencing difficulties in their studies, teachers repeated or rephrased the question or gave them more time to answer 67% of the time.

However, according to the interviews with some of the teachers, many teach from a watered-downed curriculum, knowing all along that it was designed for failure. Based on salient patterns from the interviews, 8% of the teachers felt they must be creative; for example, "As a third-grade teacher, I must become as creative as possible because of the watered-down curriculum; I take what is forbidden to teach and reverse it." Another example from a third-grade teacher, "In my classroom, I implement real-life issues as a tool to teach my students; I present to students what is familiar and move from there. I also start at the level of each student to promote academic growth by altering the school curriculum to avoid school bureaucracy for students' development." For example, "My method of teaching is to start at the level of all students and bring them up to the level where they should be." Thirty-three percent of the teachers believe that they must meet the needs of their students. One example is given from a third-grade teacher, "As a third-grade teacher, I use whatever means are necessary to secretly alter the school's curriculum to meet the needs of my students." Twenty percent of other teachers have stated, "We found a solution for this problem. We follow the school's curriculum; but, at the same time, we meet the needs of our students, making sure it is done in a discreet manner."

The comments continued. Many teachers felt that showing respect for their students' culture was a plus in academic success. They believe that since the culture of the lower-socioeconomic students of African-American and Caucasian-American origin was not included in the curriculum, these students must be respected because of their social status. One third-grade teacher and one sixth-grade teacher expressed their thoughts concerning respect for students in general, "We exercise self-respect and allow our students to express themselves in their own culture, with the understanding that we can learn from them as they learn from us." Fourteen percent of the teachers interviewed believed that open communication among teachers, students, and parents is important. A sixth-grade teacher expressed her thoughts concerning her implementation of the school curriculum, "Teaching with confidence is a display of professionalism and the expertise of a well-rounded teacher." Many teachers believe that teaching students history will allow students to be successful in school. For example, many teachers believe teaching students their true history teaches the history of a person. "History teaches where a person comes from and prevents confusion in the classroom as well in the future." One sixth-grade teacher states, "I have taught in both inner-city and suburban schools and my experience is teaching more affluent White American students and other ethnic students, but African-American male students bring something special to my classroom that has been ignored by many educators." As many as 14% of the teachers interviewed believed following the school's curriculum in the inner-city is not beneficial to students from lower-socioeconomic backgrounds. This is recognized only when it comes to teaching African-American students, not Caucasian-American students. Another sixth-grade teacher states, "In my experience, when I follow the school's curriculum, I know that my students are not successful, but I am fully aware that it is my responsibility to teach as well as to follow the school's policy and one of the policies is to teach from the school curriculum."

There were other perspectives concerning the success of students; 33% of the teachers interviewed revealed that having students work on projects was found to be essential for students to understand other cultures. Another teacher stated that she used a hidden curriculum for academic success but, according to Apple (1983) hidden curricula are not hidden at all. What these curricula teach to the majority of African-American and Caucasian-American students from lower-socioeconomic backgrounds are obedience and deference to authority, docility, subordination, extrinsic motivation, external control, dependency, and fatalism. Adoption of these behaviors ultimately predestines Black students to low-paying, low-status jobs, diminished self-concepts, and feelings of inferiority. A salient pattern for teachers continued which indicated that 33% of the teachers claimed that many students bring good morals and are eager to learn in the classroom. For example, "Many of my students bring to my classroom many different attributes, such as honesty, enthusiasm, readiness to learn, and creativity." Other teachers express the fact that many of their students also enter school to learn. For example, a teacher with ten years of experience states, "My students come to my classroom with: (a) eagerness to learn, (b) innate organizational skills at a very early age, (c) creativity, and (d) they bring their cultural expressions through speech, song, food, and moral views which I respect. Students bring enthusiasm, trust, and the willingness to learn." The last response is from a teacher who has twenty-five years of experience, "When my students enter my classroom, they come with the capability to learn." Thirty-three of the teachers indicated that their students brought many good and different skills to the classroom. For example, "Many of my students bring to my classroom good mental math skills, good artistic skills, and good verbal skills, but their skills are ignored because of the school policy." Other examples of teachers' statements concerning their students' abilities as good math students are expressed: "Many of my students bring artistic abilities and math abilities to my classroom, but they are not allowed to express them because of the school's curriculum." "Many of my male students bring to the class the ability to organize, solve complex situations, and express their ability to do mental math at an alarming rate, but the school curriculum and many teachers do not recognize these students' abilities." Many teachers felt that these students should be respected for these unique abilities that they bring to the classroom. Eight-percent of the teachers felt that it was important for teachers to recognize all students' abilities, even if they are not a part of the curriculum, because many students of African descent express their abilities in a unique manner which is misunderstood by most educators of European descent.

Salient open-ended information for Research Question 1 includes the following:

Sixth-Grade Teacher: Politics controls the educational system, but it does not control how I implement my strategies to promote academic growth among students in my classroom. A true teacher is creative; she or he uses whatever means are necessary to revolutionize the school's curriculum for academic excellence, so that boredom doesn't become mistaken for a disciplinary problem.

Third-Grade Teacher: In my classroom while teaching, I start at the level of the students and teach so they will have an understanding before I move forward.

Open-ended Question 3: Are there some special strategies and/or techniques that you as a teacher use when disciplining students of different cultures?

Sixth-Grade Teacher: In many schools, disruptive students are supposed to be sent to the principal's office; but, in most classrooms where teachers care about properly educating students, they are given outside projects. Students who are labeled as disruptive choose books of their interest and write book reports. This way, students are using their reading and mental skills through self-expression by having them place their thoughts on paper.

**Comments included:** "Students cannot learn anything positive if suspended from school." Overall, teachers stated that productive ways should be implemented to keep students in school.

Sixth-Grade Teacher: In my view, there are four philosophical beliefs as a teacher: (1) the ability to define the problem, (2) the ability to refine the problem, (3) the ability to think insightfully, and (4) the ability to be creative.

Comments included: "It was not a practical experience." The real school experience helped me to understand that there are serious problems in the infrastructure of the educational system, not only when it comes to educating students in general, but students from lower-socioeconomic backgrounds at the elementary level. They just follow the school curriculum without academic success.

"An opportunity to interview and give a school survey was helpful." The direct interviews with teachers, as a researcher, were most helpful in the search to understand the seriousness of the problems of an ineffective curriculum for students who attend school in the inner-city. Teachers should be responsible for their students' academic success and teach with respect. When it comes to teaching, it is believed by some that the present method of exposing all children to the same curriculum should be successful. Overall, teachers stated that the curriculum does include culture, backgrounds, and teaching strategies that enhance academic success.

<u>Third-Grade Teacher</u>: A third-grade teacher indicated that there are various stages that cannot be omitted when teaching: (1) students' culture and (2) students' backgrounds. "The true history must be recognized in order to prevent confusion when teaching students from the inner-city."

**Comments included**: "My experience is teaching in more affluent white American students and other ethnic groups, but African-American male students especially bring something special to my classroom that has been ignored by many educators."

It was helpful during the interview when teachers expressed their teaching strategies in their classrooms: "I understand how many teachers fail to teach toward academic success." "I understand how incorrect instructional strategies can cause academic failure in the inner-city schools by teachers' using a watered-down curriculum." "I understand how to guide teacher instructional strategies in the classroom." "I understand and apply instructional strategies which are beneficial."

Overall, many teachers stated that the reason for academic failure was not because of their inability to implement the instructional strategies, but the failure was in the realm of politics, poor curricula writers, researchers who reported negative descriptions concerning students who are from lower-socioeconomic backgrounds, attending schools in the inner-cities.

### Research Question 2

In what ways do the third- and sixth-grade level elementary students perceive that what their teachers implement from the school curriculum contributes to their academic success in school?

T-tests were run to determine whether there are differences between ways third- and sixth-grade level students perceive that what their teachers implement from the school curriculum contributes to their academic success in schools. See Table 5.

**Table 5**

**T-test for Third- and Sixth-Grade Students**

| Item | Grade Level | | Df | T | P |
| --- | --- | --- | --- | --- | --- |
| | 3rd | 6th | | | |
| 9 | 3.25 | 4.18 | 432 | -2.16 | .03 |
| 10 | 3.20 | 4.60 | 432 | -2.67 | .001 |
| 13 | 3.04 | 3.59 | 433 | -2.51 | .01 |
| 14 | 2.90 | 3.67 | 433 | -3.27 | .001 |
| 15 | 3.02 | 3.45 | 433 | -2.94 | .004 |
| 16 | 2.93 | 3.36 | 433 | -2.20 | .03 |
| 18 | 2.93 | 3.42 | 433 | -4.54 | .00 |
| 19 | 2.77 | 3.42 | 433 | -5.62 | .00 |

Note. N = 228 for 3rd grade. N = 207 for 6th grade.

** Please note that the 6th grade means are considerably higher with significant differences at **$p < 0.1$.

This table contains means, T-scores, and other values regarding grade level of students. Only the significant statistics for variables of T-values were significant at a *p (two-tailed tests) <.05 were reported.

Third-grade teachers reported higher means for items 10 (4.60), indicating that teachers give students enough time to answer a question in the classroom before calling on another student The lowest mean tabulated from the survey was item 19 (2.77). From the survey, item 19 indicated that students have a chance to show their teachers they can think through their class assignments and give different reasons why they understand their assignments.

**Table 6**

**Descriptive Statistics for Sixth-Grade Students**

| Item | Mean | Standard Deviation |
|------|------|--------------------|
| 1 | 3.45 | 1.28 |
| 2 | 3.69 | 1.07 |
| 3 | 3.63 | 1.07 |
| 4 | 3.72 | 1.07 |
| 5 | 3.63 | 1.19 |
| 6 | 3.50 | 1.15 |
| 7 | 3.52 | 1.15 |
| 8 | 3.44 | 1.24 |
| 9 | 3.50 | 1.24 |
| 10 | 3.47 | 1.22 |
| 11 | 3.43 | 1.23 |
| 12 | 3.45 | 1.20 |
| 13 | 3.40 | 1.18 |
| 14 | 3.37 | 1.18 |
| 15 | 3.33 | 1.24 |
| 16 | 3.20 | 1.26 |
| 17 | 3.40 | 1.15 |
| 18 | 3.44 | 1.16 |
| 19 | 3.42 | 1.23 |

Note: N = 216. * 1 = strongly disagree; 2 = disagree; 3 = neutral; 4 = agree; 5 = strongly agree.

Results in Table 6 showed that the highest mean was 3.72 (1 = lowest rating and 5 = highest rating); results are listed in the order of the highest mean to the lowest. The mean of item 3 (3.72) indicated that students felt that their teachers were nice to all students in the classroom. The second highest mean of item 2 (3.69) indicated that their teachers always told them to study; the third highest mean which is item 4 (3.63) indicated that students felt that their teachers wanted them to learn in all their classes.

The fourth highest, item 2 (3.50), indicated that students study to become good students. Items 6 and 9 have a mean of 3.50. Item 6 indicated that their teachers told them to work in groups, whereas item 9 (3.50) indicated that their teachers allowed them to correct their mistakes after checking their papers for the first time. Item 10 (3.47) indicated that students claimed that their teachers gave them enough time to answer questions in class before calling on another student. Item 1 (3.45) indicated that the students claimed that they were always told by their teachers to study. Item 18 (3.44) indicated that students claimed that their teachers made sure they understand all their materials before moving to the next section. Item 11 (3.43) indicated that students were given a chance to correct their mistakes and give their papers back to their teachers for further comments. Item 19 (3.42) indicated that students claimed that they had a chance to show their teachers that they could think through their class assignments and give different reasons why; whereas, the lowest mean, on item 16 (3.20), indicated that students were able to understand more when their teachers worked with them.

## Qualitative

Weber (1994) suggested ways for students to learn and that is for teachers to motivate their students by offering them support and friendship.

According to the interviews with students at the third- and sixth-grade levels, few students have the privilege to experience such care in the classroom. For example, one third-grade student stated, "I'm a good reader, I type and I'm good in math, although my grades are very poor; my teacher just doesn't like me because she knows that I'm good in math; she wants to kill my spirit, but she will never do that." A sixth-grade male student expressed his thoughts concerning how he is treated in the classroom, "I can work three problem-solving problems to my teacher's one. My teacher has to go the teacher's manual to show the class how to work out these types of problem when I can do them mentally; this she does not like. She wants to set up equations that makes no sense at all. Many of the students get confused, and when I try to help them the teacher gets mad. We spend forty-five minutes doing one problem using unnecessary steps to do this easy math.

A third-grade female expressed how she was treated in the classroom, "There are no special things that my teacher does for me to succeed; all my teacher does is yell at the top of her lungs." Another female student in the sixth grade stated, "I have heard many of my classmates say that their teachers are nice, but I have two questions to ask. Does nice teach students advance work? Does nice teach students how to study? The answer to these two questions are □no,' not at this or in any classroom. Nice in this school has nothing to do with educating Black students.

Some students think a good teacher is fair; I don't think so. If a teacher is fair, that teacher would be fair and honest, honest enough not to cheat Black students out of a good education. This is what is going on at this school. We are being cheated and trained. If we as students were being taught, we would be given the opportunity to think, we as students would be learning how to make decisions and be prepared by our teachers for higher thinking."

Salient open-ended information for Research Question 2 includes the following:

Open-ended Question 1: Tell me what you think makes a good classroom teacher.

Third-Grade Student: A good teacher is one who will be nice to all students, let us play special games in the classroom. A good teacher is one who is fair and teaches us things that we do not understand and not yell all the time when we raise our hand to ask questions.

**Comments included:** "Students are wise enough to know when and what they are learning that will be effective for them at the next level." Overall third-grade students come to school to learn, and they are enthusiastic when a teacher is teaching them.

**Open-ended Question 2**: What unique qualities do you as a student bring into your third- or sixth-grade classroom?

**Sixth-Grade Student:** Math, science, and music, but in science, they do not do experiments in class that I see students on television participating in. Students are entering science fairs and presenting their projects to the nation. The teacher states that the school does not have funding for insurance to cover students for such programs.

**Third-Grade Student No. 1**: I'm a good reader and I can read maps and I like geography and health.

**Third-Grade Student No. 2:** I don't know, we do the same thing every day.

**Third-Grade Student No. 3:** No, it is the same ole thing, write one hundred lines (I will not disrupt the class). This is not special. Many of the students are asking the teachers questions. The teacher gets bent out of shape and starts threatening to send students to the principal's office.

## Research Question 3

To what extent is the difference between what the teachers implement and what students perceive as being implemented representative of school curricula in third- and sixth-grade level classroom settings?

**Quantitative**

### Table 7

### Descriptive Statistics for Sixth-Grade Teachers

| Item | Mean | Standard Deviation |
|------|------|--------------------|
| 1 | 4.75 | .46 |
| 5 | 4.13 | 1.36 |
| 6 | 3.75 | 1.49 |
| 16 | 3.88 | 1.55 |
| 8 | 3.88 | 1.55 |
| 9 | 4.13 | 1.13 |
| 17 | 4.25 | .49 |

Note. N = 216. 1 = strongly disagree; 2 = disagree; 3 = neutral; 4 = agree; and 5 = strongly agree. A T-test was run to determine the differences between the relationship of what teachers implement and the perception of what students perceive between third- and sixth-grade levels. See Table 7.

Results of the table revealed that students at the sixth-grade level had no significant difference in the ways students perceive what their teachers implement from school curricula at the third- and sixth-grade levels. The mean scores for six of the items suggest a difference in the following areas: (1) treatment of students, (2) interaction more with male than female students, (3) encouraging students to study, (4) discipline problems, (5) giving students opportunities to work in groups, and (6) using more worksheets than textbooks. However, there were no real differences. For example, the mean score on the treatment of students was 4.42 and the mean for teachers interacting more with male students than female was 4.42. The mean for giving students the opportunity to work in groups was 4.42; for students using more ditto sheets in the classroom than textbooks, the mean was 4.71. For discipline prohibits, the mean was 4.57.

## Qualitative

Many insufficiencies of school curricula were implemented by teachers to students who attend school in the inner-cities. Inner-city school teachers gave more directions, criticized their students more, asked fewer questions, and accepted or clarified students' ideas less frequently. These teachers' behavior related negatively to students from lower-socioeconomic backgrounds. Perkins (1985) confirms that students from the inner-city fail at the elementary level which related to withdrawal on the part of the student and criticism on the part the teacher. In contrast, many teachers indicated that they are least prepared to teach because the school curriculum was designed to fail students from lower-socioeconomic backgrounds (Kunjufu,1985). These results are consistent with the studies of (Comer,1989) and (Frisby,1992) that teachers implement a school curriculum in an unproductive manner. Good & Dembo (1973) found that 93% of teachers called students from lower-socioeconomic backgrounds to answer questions that required them only to recall information. They were given few opportunities to practice higher-level thinking. Bloom (1984) and Tractenberg (1974) have stated that textbooks emphasize specific content to be remembered and give students little opportunity to use higher-level skills, such as giving opinions, assessing facts, drawing implications, evaluating information or facts. But, according to the answers to the survey questionnaire and the answers from the interviews with students, there were discrepancies concerning perception on the part of teachers.

Based on the salient pattern found in the response to the interview questions from students, 14% of the students at the third- and sixth-grade levels revealed that clarity, self-expression, not believing lies told by other teachers, and implementing materials conducive to learning are attributes to describe a good teacher. For example, "A good teacher is one who can explain subjects with clarity; not only that, a good teacher must have a sense of humor." Other students revealed that a good teacher is one who can explain math or any other subject to students without confusion. A good teacher is one who will not listen to other teachers when describing a student as one with behavior problems. For example, one student stated students are said to have behavior problems when, in reality, these students are just bored to death because the teacher teaches the same subjects the same way over and over again, going over the same things that students already know. Many students expressed to the interviewer, for example, "We want to do work that will allow us to think and express ourselves so we can excel as other students at Ivy League Schools." We do not get the opportunity to express ourselves. We are just as smart as other students in this state. We want to become attorneys but we know the way we are being taught; we won't be able to enter any college with high ranking unless we pass the SAT Test with high scores, and that is why we are studying for high SAT scores. Many of us study on our own. My aunt and many other students have families who give us good pointers on how to study and we share these pointers with other students who are interested in studying with us." Fourteen-percent of the students believed that encouragement from teachers is a good sign of a quality teacher. For example, "A good teacher is one who encourages students to build their self-esteem, as well as be fair and supportive of students in all their academic endeavors."

Salient open-ended information for Research Question 3 includes the following:

**Open-ended Question 4**: In what ways are the classroom subjects that you are learning in your classroom useful in your life?

**Sixth-Grade Student:** Nothing. If I quit school at the six grade level and have children, I'll teach them how to read from a second-grade reader. I can teach my children to read when they attend Head Start. In this school we are taught to fail. The only thing we are being educated for is to become dependable citizens, living on the crumbs of society.

You would think that someone had this in mind when teachers come in this school to train rather than to teach.

**Sixth-Grade Teacher**: As a teacher, I allow my students to work in groups so they can learn how to work with other students who are not able to work alone without complications.

## Research Question 4

To what extent do teachers implement their instruction strategies for African-American and Caucasian-American students from lower-socioeconomic backgrounds at the third- and sixth-grade levels for academic success in schools in the Midwest and southern part of the United States?

## Quantitative

### Table 8
### One-Way ANOVA for Students

| Item | DF | F | P |
|------|------|------|-----|
| 2 | 436 | 3.80 | .01 |
| 3 | 436 | 4.43 | .00 |
| 5 | 436 | 9.39 | .00 |
| 6 | 436 | 5.33 | .00 |
| 7 | 436 | 3.02 | .07 |
| 8 | 436 | 3.50 | .02 |
| 9 | 436 | 3.15 | .05 |
| 10 | 436 | 5.48 | .00 |
| 11 | 436 | 6.91 | .00 |
| 12 | 436 | 5.14 | .00 |
| 13 | 439 | 3.40 | .03 |
| 14 | 439 | 3.58 | .02 |
| 15 | 439 | 3.88 | .01 |
| 16 | 439 | 3.53 | .02 |
| 17 | 439 | 4.56 | .00 |
| 19 | 439 | 4.62 | .00 |

Note: Only the significant items were reported at $**p < .01$.
Items: 2, 3, 5, 6, 7, 8, 9, 10, 11, 12, 13, 14, 15, 16, 17, and 19 were
   significant.

A one-way analysis of variance test was used to compare schools in the Midwest and schools in the Southern portion of the United States. Results in Tables 7 and 8 indicated there were significant differences between schools in the Midwest and the southern portion of the United States. Students at the BWC School in the southern portion of the United States believed their teachers make classroom rules clear, whereas teachers in the Midwest teach clarity and classroom rules less. There is a significant difference between schools in the southern portion of the United States when it comes to item 19 where students think they have a chance to show their teachers they can think through and explain why concerning their classroom work.

Item 12 indicated that students in the southern portion of the United States receive clear directions at the beginning of each class session, whereas student in the Midwest don't.

There are no differences between item 11 in the southern portion of the United States and item 11 in the Midwest when it comes to students' receiving positive comments from their teacher. Schools in the Midwest also have a significant difference when it comes to item 3. In the southern portion of the United States, students think their teachers are fair. In item 4 for students, they think their teachers make the classroom rules clear.

There are no significant differences in item 4 where students thought their teachers want the best for them.

## Qualitative

In order to meet the academic needs of students in one school in a Midwestern town, it chose to allow representatives of the Edison Project, a New York-Based Corporation, to come in to manage the school's curriculum. The Edison Project, founded in 1991, is a private manager of public schools. The company claims it can increase student performance and turn a profit for the same cost per pupil that the school district already allocates. The school districts would contract with Edison, which comes in to implement the school's curriculum. In the southern portion of the state, schoolteachers use hidden curricula to meet the needs of their students; but, in most cases, according to Apple (1983) hidden curricula for teaching students from lower-socioeconomic backgrounds are not in the best interest of poor students. This curriculum implements in the classroom for the majority of students from lower-socioeconomic backgrounds is obedience and deference to authority, docility, subordination, extrinsic motivation, external control, dependence, and fatalism. Adoption of these behaviors ultimately predestines African-American and Caucasian-American students from lower-socioeconomic backgrounds to low-paying, low-status jobs, diminished self-concepts, and feelings of inferiority. Anyon and Rist provided illuminating examples of just how these hidden curricula operate. School where African-American and Caucasian-American students from lower-socioeconomic backgrounds attend in the inner-cities, as described by Anyon (1981), reflect the lack of initiative, hierarchy, and inflexibility. From these curricula, teachers routinely gave students work, with no explanation of its relevance or purpose to life or to previous assignments.

**Table 9**

**Descriptive Statistics for Race (Caucasian-American and other minority Students)**

| Item | Means | Standard Deviation |
|------|-------|--------------------|
| 2    | 3.66  | 1.11               |
| 3    | 3.53  | 1.14               |
| 4    | 3.66  | 1.17               |
| 5    | 3.00  | 1.19               |

Note: N = 96. This table contains means and standard deviations regarding level of students only the significant statistics were reported.

Results in Table 9 show that the highest mean was on items 2 and 4, respectively (2 = highest and 5 = lowest rating), indicating that students studied to be good students and item 4 students think that their teacher wants the best for them. Item 3 students think that their teachers are fair with all students. The lowest mean is item 5 which indicated that students claim that their teachers make the classroom rules clear at the beginning of the school year.

**Table 10**

**Descriptive Statistics for Race (African-American Students)**

| Item | Means | Standard Deviation |
|------|-------|--------------------|
| 1    | 3.00  | 1.20               |
| 2    | 3.19  | 1.19               |
| 17   | 2.62  | 1.09               |
| 19   | 3.20  | 1.24               |

Note: N = 229. This table contains means and standard regarding level of students. Only the significant statistics were reported.

Results in Table 10 show that the highest mean was item 19 (3.20) (1 = lowest and 5 = highest rating), that students had a chance to show their teachers thay could think through their work. Item 2 indicated that students studied to be good students and item 17 indicated that students worked from textbooks rather than dittos in the classroom.

**Table 11**

**Descriptive Statistics for Female Students**

| Item | Mean | Standard Deviation |
|------|------|--------------------|
| 1    | 3.57 | 1.37               |
| 2    | 3.62 | 1.15               |
| 4    | 3.60 | 1.21               |
| 16   | 3.04 | 1.21               |

Note: N=221. This table contains means and standard deviations regarding grade level of students. Only the significant statistics were reported.

Results in Table 11 showed that the highest mean was item 2 (3.62) (1 = lowest rating and 5 = highest rating). The response of students indicated that they study to be good students. The next highest, item 4 (3.63), indicated that students felt that their teachers wanted the best for them. The third highest mean was item 1 (3.57), which indicated that the students' teachers encouraged their students in the classroom, and the lowest, item 16 (3.04), indicated that students understood more.

## Quantitative Summary

The quantitative data for the study suggest that there were few significant differences between third- and sixth-grade teachers when it came to implementing strategies for their students. However, as for teachers' implementations and what students perceive what their teachers implement, there were significant differences between third- and sixth-graders. Regarding the students' geographical areas, there were significant differences between the race of students; however, there were no significant differences between the gender of students.

# CHAPTER X

# PERSONAL INTERVIEWS

From a qualitative perspective for the study, personal interviews were conducted with fourteen teachers and ten students. All subjects are teachers who teach third- and sixth-grade students. The interview questions for teachers and students were collected using written notes and transcribed by the researcher.

The teacher interviews lasted between thirty and forty-five minutes; nine of the students's interviews lasted less than fourteen minutes, with one student interview lasting approximately one hour. The fourteen teacher subjects (nine females and five males) responded to questions categorized under the following topics: (a) philosophical beliefs as a teacher, (b) unique characteristics that students bring to the classroom, (c) strategies and techniques teachers use in the classroom, (d) potential mismatch between what teachers want to teach and what the administration wants them to teach, and (e) what ways teachers are successful when working with students from various socioeconomic and cultural backgrounds.

Ten students (five males and five females) responded to questions categorized under the following topics: (a) tell me what you think makes a good teacher, (b) what unique features do you as a student bring to the classroom, (c) what special things does your teacher do in the classroom when disciplining disruptive students, and (d) in what ways are the subjects that you are learning in your classroom useful in life?

The researcher first focused on all interview questions for teachers' philosophical beliefs, teaching strategies, students' characteristics brought to the classroom and how teachers teach students from various socioeconomic and cultural backgrounds.

All subjects talked freely since the interviews were not tape recorded. When talking about their philosophical beliefs, six of the subjects seemed hostile as represented by their comments. The general consensus of these six subjects was concerned with the fact that their white co-workers were not prepared to teach students of African-American descent. They appeared hostile when giving their comments. but, as the interviews progressed, it appeared that the subjects were not as hostile toward their white co-workers. It appeared they realized society was at fault for their negative feelings and began to turn their anger into positive views for the sake of their students who were in school to be educated.

The following subjects (teachers) are representative of the fourteen females and one male who covered all five interview questions. The researcher selected fictitious names of Odell, Sarah, Ceria, Edie, Sean, Regina, Dorothy, Connie, Linda, Marilyn, Marian, Melissa, Tanya, Mattie, and Shelley. It should be noted that these excerpts are pieced together from much longer transcribed interviews.

Fictitious names were used for ten students' subjects (five males and five females) who were interviewed. The researcher selected names of Eric, Alfred, Jordan, Tony, Charles, Pam, Rosa, Chama, Cassandra, Tara and Noly for these students. "Q" means researcher's question and "R" means the subject's response.

Odell.     Q: Tell me something about your philosophical beliefs as a teacher.
           R: When teaching students, various stages cannot be omitted, regardless of the student's social and cultural backgrounds, because it is the universal order of teaching: (a) teachers should love their students if they are going to represent the teaching profession, and (b) teachers must have the desire to teach without malice in their hearts toward any student.

Ronnie     Q: What kind of unique characteristics do you believe your students bring to the classroom?
           R: My students are at the third-grade level when they enter my classroom. They bring many different attributes, such as honesty, enthusiasm, readiness to learn, and creativity. When students leave home for school at a young age, they are filled with a special ray in their mannerism which indicates they are eager to learn. At the elementary level, students have capacity to grasp an abundance of knowledge at an early age. This is why it is very important for teachers to be well-prepared to teach young students; these young students are delicate in spirit and this spirit can be easily broken if the wrong person stands before them wearing a mask of deception.
           Q: Are there some strategies and/or techniques that you as a teacher use when disciplining students of different cultures?
           R: There is a difference between a disciplinary problem and boredom. When it comes to students, particularly those of African-American descent, males particularly, I find boredom rather than a disciplinary problem. My strategy eliminates this problem of boredom when I exercise understanding and alter the school's curriculum by giving students work that consists of materials that are advanced which allow them to use the knowledge already acquired for grounds to excel. Colleges and universities are not preparing future elementary education teachers to understand human behavior when it comes to African-American and Caucasian-American students from

59

lower-socioeconomic backgrounds. Without the true understanding of all cultures and human behavior as an elementary education teacher, there will always be a misconception between what is a disciplinary problem and boredom.

Q: How do you handle the potential mismatch between what you want to teach and what the administration wants you to teach?

R: As a third-grade teacher, I must become as creative as possible. From the school's curriculum, I take what is forbidden to teach in reverse.

Q: What ways are you successful when working with students from various socioeconomic and culture backgrounds?

R: I exercise self-respect, as well as respecting all my students' cultures. I allow my students to express themselves in their own culture with the understanding that we all can learn from each other.

Sarah.

Q: Tell me something about your philosophical beliefs as a teacher.

R: Every child has a constitutional right to an equal and proper education. Teachers in general should be responsible to find workable teaching strategies which are conducive to each student so that each student can excel at his or her own rate of learning, whether in the inner-city or suburban classrooms.

Q: What kinds of unique characteristics do you believe your students bring to the classroom?

R: Many of my students bring to my classroom good artistic skills as craftsmen, good verbal skills, and good mental mathematics skills. These skills are ignored because of the school's policies.

Q: Are there some strategies and/or techniques that you do as a teacher when disciplining students of different culture?

R: In the school where I teach, disruptive students are supposed to be sent to the principal's office; but, in my classroom, I allow students who are labeled as disruptive students to choose books of their interest and do a book report. This way students are using their reading and mental skills through self-expression by them placing on paper.

Q: How do you handle the potential mismatch between what you want to teach and what the administration wants you to teach?

R: In my classroom, I implement real-life issues as a tool to teach my students. I present to them what is familiar and move from there.

Q: In what ways are you successful when working with students from various socioeconomic and cultural backgrounds?

R: Respect must be exhibited between both teacher and students. I allow my students to have self-expression in the classroom; self-expression allows students to bond with me as their teacher and their classmates, resulting in academic success.

Q: Tell me something about your philosophical beliefs as a teacher.

R: Teachers should implement to students in the classroom humane and ethical ways for students to give back to their community. Every child can learn, unless the child is dead. Many teachers claim certain students in this country cannot learn because they are from a certain ethnic background; this is not true.

Q: What kinds of unique characteristics do you believe your students bring to the classroom?

R: Students come to my classroom with: (1) an eagerness to learn, (2) innate organizational skills at a very early ages, (3) creativity, and (4) they bring their cultural expressions through speech, song, foods, and morals views which I respect.

Q: Are there some strategies and/or techniques that you as a teacher use when disciplining students of different cultures?

R: I listen to my students' understanding of their needs and try to meet their needs accordingly; working with them, trying to meet their needs, allows them to be productive in the future.

Q: How do you handle the potential mismatch between what you want to teach and what the administration wants you to teach?

R: My method of teaching is to start at the level of the students and bring the students up to the level where they should be.

Q: In what ways are you successful when working with students from various socioeconomic and cultural backgrounds?

R: Teaching is an art; I keep a line of communication open between myself, students and parents. I implement caring, student/teacher morale, academic support, and team work.

Ceria

Q: Tell me something about your philosophical beliefs as a teacher.

R: In my view, there are four philosophical beliefs as a teacher: (1) the ability to define the problem, (2) the ability to redefine the problem, (3) the ability to think insightfully, and (4) the ability to be creative.

Q: What kinds of unique characteristics do you believe your students being to the classroom?

R: Students come to school with unique attributes; in my classroom, my students bring: (1) common courtesy, (2) honesty, (3) trust, (4) innocence, and (4) most of all, insight.

Q: Are there some strategies and or techniques that you as a teacher use when disciplining students of different cultures?

R: Since I teach sixth grade, one strategy that I use in my classroom is to take students at face value. I use what the student is doing to be disruptive in the classroom as a learning tool for the student. For the next meeting session, I have that student prepare and teach the subject disrupted in that class, by lecturing, and grade that student accordingly for that entire year. The students will know at an early date if failure is in the future for them.

Q: How do you handle the potential mismatch between what you want to teach and what the administration wants you to teach?

R: Although politics controls the educational system, it does not control how I implement my strategies to promote academic growth among students in my classroom. A true teacher is creative, using whatever means are necessary to revolutionize the school's curriculum for academic excellence, so that boredom doesn't become mistaken for a behavior problem.

Q: In what ways are you successful when working with students from various socioeconomic and cultural backgrounds?

R: Busing works well for students from different socioeconomic backgrounds and cultures; it makes it easy for all students to bond because of the circumstances which they have to endure to complete the project. By creating productive projects for teamwork, students learn to work together well for the completion of the project.

Edie

Q: Tell me something about your philosophical beliefs as a teacher.

R: There are various stages that cannot be omitted when teaching: (1) teaching of students' culture and (2) omit students' backgrounds.

Q: What kinds of unique characteristics do you believe your students bring to the classroom?

R: Many of my students bring artistic ability, mathematical skills, creativity and organizational skills to my classroom, but they are not allowed to express them because of the school's curriculum.

Q: Are there some strategies and/or techniques you as a teacher use when disciplining students of different culture?

R: No, I follow the school's policy and send disruptive students to the principal's office.

Q: How do you handle the potential mismatch between what you want to teach and what the administration wants you to teach?

R: There is nothing to handle; I just follow the school's curriculum.

Q: In what ways are you successful when working with students from various socioeconomic and culture backgrounds?

R: Academically, none; as a coach, I'm able to teach life skills.

Q: Tell me something about your philosophical beliefs as a teacher.

R: All children can learn, and teachers should always seek ways to improve their teaching strategies or skills.

Q: What kinds of unique characteristics do you believe your students bring to the classroom?

R: For the females, good penmanship; for the males, mathematical skills.

Q: Are there some strategies and/or techniques that you as a teacher use when disciplining students of different cultures?

R: No, I follow the school policies, such as in-school suspension, school suspension for several days, or year suspension.

Q: How do you handle the potential mismatch between what you want to teach and what the administration wants you to teach?

R: As a teacher, I follow the curriculum provided by the school.

Q: In what ways are successful when working with students from various socioeconomic and cultural backgrounds?

R: When following this school's curriculum, there is no success.

Regina　　Q: Tell me something about your philosophical beliefs as a teacher.

R: Teachers should be responsible for their students' academic success and teach with respect.

Q: What kinds of unique characteristics do you believe your students bring to the classroom?

R: Many of my students bring enthusiasm, trust, and the willingness to learn.

Q: Are there some strategies and/or techniques that you as a teacher use when disciplining students of different cultures?

R: In the school where I teach, disruptive students are to report to the principal's office; but, instead, I give students who are disruptive a class assignment which consists of writing a composition that must contain a solution for their disruption.

Q: How do you handle the potential mismatch between what you want to teach and what the administration wants you to teach?

R: As an experienced teacher, I understand how to avoid the bureaucracy of the school policy. I do not worry about what the administrators want; many of them have never taught in a

63

classroom. What do they know about teaching? Many administrators should listen to what many good teaches have to say and follow their suggestions. Many problems in schools lie at the feet of the administration, poor teachers, poor principals and bad politicians, not the students. I teach students what is beneficial for my students. I teach for the future; my methods of teaching will give them a solid background at the elementary level, so they can be well-prepared for advanced classes.

Q: In what ways are you successful when working with students from various socioeconomic and cultural backgrounds?

R: Teaching students their true history teaches the history of a person. History teaches where a person came from and prevents confusion in the future. I have taught in both inner-city and suburban schools and my experiences are with teaching more affluent white American students and other ethnic groups; but, African-American male students bring something special to my classroom that has been ignored by many educators.

Norman   Q: Tell me something about your philosophical beliefs as a teacher.

R: Every child has a constitutional right to be properly educated. Teachers should be fair toward students when it comes to students' expressing themselves in all their abilities.

Q: What kinds of unique characteristics do you believe your students bring to the classroom?

R: Many of my students bring to my class the ability to organize and solve complex situations and express their ability to do mental mathematics at an alarming rate; but, the school curriculum does not allow these students to express these abilities. The school's curriculum rejects these abilities by enforcing traditional standards for teaching.

Q: Are there some strategies and/or techniques that you as a teacher use when disciplining students of different cultures?

R: Community assignments are given to those students who disrupt my classroom. The assignment is to visit the local unemployment office and write a paper concerning what they observed and report back to the classroom.

Q: How do you handle the potential mismatch between what you want to teach and what the administration wants you to teach?

R: I do not worry about what the administration wants; many of them have never taught in a classroom. What do they know about teaching? Many administrators should listen to what many of the "good" teachers have to say and follow their suggestions.

Many problems in the schools lie at the feet of the administration, poor teachers, poor principals and bad politicians, not the students. What is not understood by poor teachers is that they do not know that the system is wrong. This is why they are afraid to do their job even though they have control of their classroom.

Q: In what ways are you successful when working with students from various socioeconomic and cultural backgrounds?

R: Teaching is a craft; this is why I give assignments which call for teamwork.

Dorothy   Q: Tell me something about your philosophical beliefs as a teacher.

R: All teachers should treat students with respect and forget about what administration dictates to them.

Q: What kinds of unique characteristics do you believe your students bring to the classroom?

R: When students enter my classroom, they come with the capability to learn.

Q: Are there some strategies and/or techniques that you as a teacher use when disciplining students of different cultures?

R: In my classroom, I exercise love toward my students. Many teachers have a difficult time mistaking disciplinary problems from boredom. This creates problems, not only for teachers, but most importantly for students, particularly for the African-American male students who are from lower-socioeconomic backgrounds.

Q: How do you handle the potential mismatch between what you want to teach and what the administration wants you to teach?

R: In my classroom while teaching, I start at the level of the students and teach so that they will have an understanding before I move forward.

Q: In what ways are you successful when working with students from various socioeconomic and cultural backgrounds?

R: Working with students in general, I allow them to work as a team. This method allows students to learn from each other.

Marilyn   Q: Tell me about your philosophical beliefs as a teacher.

R: There is a universal order of teaching, and love for students is the greatest of all.

Q: What kinds of unique characteristic do you believe your students bring to the classroom?

R: When students leave home for school, they are filled with the eagerness to learn. They bring with them trust, honesty, and common courtesy.

Q: Are there some strategies and/or techniques that you as a teacher use when disciplining students of different cultures?

R: I'm sorry to say that I must follow school's policy when it comes to disciplining students. The policy of our school is to send disruptive students to the principal's office.

Q: How do you handle the potential mismatch between what you want to teach and what the administration wants you to teach?

R: I must say that it is my job to follow school's policy and that is to teach according to the school's curriculum.

Q: In what ways are you successful when working with students from various socioeconomic and cultural backgrounds?

R: I never taught in a school where there was diversity in students, only in faculty.

Sallie

Q: Tell me something about your philosophical beliefs as a teacher.

R: Teachers should learn the history of all students so that harmony is kept in the classroom among teacher and students.

Q: What kinds of unique characteristics do you believe your students bring to the classroom?

R: When children enter school, they become students. Within every one of these students comes unique attributes that "God" has given to each of them: (1) love, (2) honesty, (3) trust, and (4) innocence. With these attributes, students use them in the most productive manner one can ever imagine; but, most teachers come with their negative attitudes, labeling students' attributes as behavior problems.

Q: Are there some strategies and/or techniques that you as a teacher use when disciplining students of different cultures?

R: In the public school system many cases that appear to teachers as disciplinary problems are merely mistaken boredom. This conversation has been addressed in my school concerning a student who has been labeled as a student with disciplinary problem; but, when I studied the student, I found the student to be bright. The student was just bored because of the classroom structure. The student was far more advanced than his classmates. When he finished his work, he would begin to disturb others in the classroom. So you see, boredom in this case has been mistaken for a disciplinary problem. I give this student extra work, not send him to the principal's office.

Q: How do you handle the potential mismatch between what you want to teach and what the administration wants you to teach?

R: As a teacher, I use whatever means are necessary to secretly: alter the school's curriculum to fit the needs of my students.

Q: In what ways are you successful when working with students from various socioeconomic and cultural backgrounds?

R: As a teacher, I allow my students to work in groups so that they can learn how to work with other students who are not quite as advanced or are from other backgrounds. This way students can learn from each other.

Melissa.   Q: Tell me something about your philosophical beliefs as a teacher.

R: Fairness should be exercised among teachers and students. Teachers should keep a line of communication open for students.

Q: What kinds of unique characteristics do you believe your students bring to the classroom?

R: Many of my students have organizational and mental mathematical skills.

Q: Are there some strategies and/or techniques that you as a teacher use when disciplining students of different cultures?

R: Since my students have good mental math and organizational skills, I allow them to work in groups when solving problems.

Q: How do you handle the potential mismatch between what you want to teach and what the administration wants you to teach?

R: I found a solution for this problem. I follow the curriculum; but, at the same time, I meet the needs of my students.

Q: In what ways are you successful when working with students from various socioeconomic and cultural backgrounds?

R: I find many of my techniques work well with all students when allowed to do group work in the classroom; students can bond with each other as well.

Tanya.   Q: Tell me something about your philosophical beliefs as a teacher.

R: Teachers should have more that one strategy to teach students. Teachers should be fair and honest with their students.

Q: What kinds of unique characteristics do you believe your students bring to the classroom?

R: Well, I must say in my classroom I find a gender split. Most of the males are very good in math, science and technology; as for the females, they have good verbal qualities, penmanship, and spelling. This not to say that the females are not good in math, science and technology, but it seems to it take females longer to solve the math problems in my classroom.

Q: Are there some strategies and/or techniques that you as a teacher use when disciplining students of different cultures?

R: My students are well behaved; I keep them busy.

Q: How do you handle the potential mismatch between what you want to teach and what the administration wants you to teach?

R: I have no problem with the subjects that I want to teach; I meet the needs of my students and not the needs of the administration.

Q: In what ways are you successful when working with students from various socioeconomic and cultural backgrounds?

R: Success comes when a teacher is confident in what she or he is doing.

Mattie.

Q: Tell me something about your philosophical beliefs as a teacher.

R: Teachers should encourage their students. There should be teacher-student relationships, and teachers should encourage students to learn from each other.

Q: What kinds of unique characteristics do you believe your students bring to the classroom?

R: In my classroom, students demonstrate a connection with each other which tells me there are communication skills and that these students can be competitive achievers.

Q: Are there some strategies and/or techniques that you as a teacher use when disciplining students of different cultures?

R: Yes. First, I talk "to" the student and, secondly, I talk "with" the student, keeping a positive attitude.

Q: How do you handle the potential mismatch between what you want to teach and what the administration wants you to teach?

R: I have no problem teaching what is beneficial for the students.

Q: In what ways are you successful when working with students from various socioeconomic and cultural backgrounds?

R: When it comes to teaching, success comes with the professional experience and the expertise of the teacher.

Clara.

Q: Tell me something about your philosophical beliefs as a teacher.

R: Teachers should maintain positive attitudes when it comes to teaching. Sitting before them there are many students with many different personalities, bringing with them many different rates for learning.

Q: What kinds of unique characteristics do you believe your students being to the classroom?

R: Students are unique within themselves. Coming to school to learn, they bring enthusiasm.

Q: Are there some strategies and or/or techniques that you as a teacher use when disciplining students of different cultures?

R: No, I treat all students with respect.

Q: How do you handle the potential mismatch between what you want to teach and what the administration wants you to teach?

R: I teach to meet the needs of the students.

Q: In what ways are you successful when working with students from various socioeconomic and cultural backgrounds?

R: Keeping a positive attitude and having confidence in yourself as a teacher.

Marain.

Q: Tell me something about your philosophical beliefs as a teacher.

R: Teachers must respect students as people, too. They must show this respect verbally as well as with their body language.

Q: What kinds of unique characteristics do you believe your students bring to the classroom?

R: When students enter my classroom, each brings something special and that is a different personality, different rate in which each learns. When I teach, I keep this in mind.

Q: Are there some strategies and /or techniques that you as a teacher use when disciplining students of different cultures?

R: No, the majority of students are all alike when it comes to behavior. This is what many teachers do not understand. All students can misbehave sometimes, but in different ways. Teachers must be experienced enough to know how to handle these small problems before they get out of hand.

Q: How do you handle the potential mismatch between what you want to teach and what the administration wants you to teach?

R: I have no problem teaching what I want to teach; I control my classroom.

Q: In what ways are you successful when working with students from various socioeconomic and cultural backgrounds?

R: I listen, communicate, and treat each student as an individual.

Shelly.

Q: Tell me something about your philosophical beliefs as a teacher.

R: Teachers must treat students as children and not as adults they must remember that students are not developed as adults and haveless experience when it comes to giving directions. This is why directions should given to students with self-discipline by teachers.

Q: What kinds of unique characteristics do you believe your students bring to the classroom?

R: Students are eager to learn without malice.

Q: Are there some strategies and or techniques that you as a teacher use when disciplining students of different cultures?

R: No.

Q: How do you handle the potential mismatch between what you want to teach and what the administration wants you to teach?

R: I just follow the school's curriculum.

Q: In what ways are you successful when working with students from various socioeconomic and cultural backgrounds?

R: Having my students work on a project that calls for cooperation by all students before the project can be completed.

## STUDENT INTERVIEWS

Eric

Q: Tell me what you think makes a good classroom teacher.

R: A good teacher is one who can explain subjects with clarity not only that, a good teacher must have a sense of humor.

Q: What unique features do you, as a student, bring into your third- or sixth-grade classroom?

R: Typing, giving good reports, drama, and I'm an excellent reader.

Q: Are there special things that your teacher does in the classroom when disciplining disruptive students?

R: No.

Q: In what ways are the classroom subjects that you are learning in your classroom useful in your life?

R: Since I am an excellent reader and can take good notes, these skills can land me a job as a news reporter or a school teacher. If I were to become a school teacher, I would not treat students the way teachers treat students at this school. I would have patience and remember that I was once a student.

Alfred.

Q: Tell me what you think makes a good classroom teacher.

R: A good teacher is one who can encourage students to build their self-esteem, as well as be fair and be supportive to students in all their academic endeavors.

Q: What unique features do you, as a student, bring into your third- or sixth-grade classroom?

R: I am a good artist, but my teacher does not encourage me in every way to explore my horizons in this field. When I tell her I

70

want to be a free lance artist, she tells me that I would make a good carpenter. I think this is wrong for her to tell me this. There should be encouragement coming from my teacher, not discouragement, because I know what I want to be, but I will not put all my eggs in one basket.

Q: Are there special things that your teacher does in the classroom when disciplining disruptive students?

R: No. If any of the boys try to ask questions in class, our teacher would tell us to be quiet, if not, she will send us to the principal's office.

Q: In what ways are the classroom subjects that you are learning in your classroom useful in your life?

R: Well, in order to be a free lance artist, math is essential and our teacher is poor in math. I guess I can became a teacher or an engineer.

Marvin.  Q: Tell me what you think makes a good teacher.

R: A good teacher is one who has good teaching abilities, considers the educational interests of students, and is fair.

Q: What unique features do you, as a student, bring into your third- or sixth-grade classroom?

R: I'm a good science, math, and technology student in the sixth grade.

Q: Are there special things that your teacher does in the classroom when disciplining disruptive students?

R: No. It is the same old thing, write a hundred lines, (I will not disrupt the class). This is not special. Many of the students are asking the teacher for certain information of their interest. She gets bent out of shape and starts threatening to send us to the principal's office.

Q: In what ways are the classroom subjects that you are learning in your classroom useful in your life?

R: Math, science, and computers. Since being a good math student is the gateway to becoming a great mathematician like Albert Einstein, I think I will be able to work as a medical researcher.

Tony.  Q: Tell me what you think makes a good classroom teacher.

R: A good teacher is nice and lets us play special games in the classroom.

Q: What unique features do you, as a student, bring into your third- or sixth-grade classroom?

71

R: In the third grade, we draw a lot. I could draw and color good when I was in the second grade; now I can draw and color better.

Q: What does your teacher do in the classroom when disciplining disruptive students?

R: She gives us time out.

Q: In what ways are the classroom subjects that you are learning in your classroom useful in your life?

R: I want to be a nurse when I grow up, or a doctor. Since I can draw, maybe I can work in the library where they keep paintings.

Charles.

Q: Tell me what you think makes a good teacher.

R: A good teacher is one who gives constructive criticism, has a positive attitude, and can communicate well with students under stress.

Q: What unique features do you, as a student, bring into your third- or sixth-grade classroom?

R: I'm a good reader, I have a good relationship with my peers, I type, and I'm good in math. My grades are very poor, but this doesn't bother me because I have a mother who has faith in me and I have faith in myself. When I go to high school, my grades will improve. My teacher just doesn't like me because she knows I'm good in math; she wants to kill my spirit, but she will never do that.

Q: Are there special things that your teacher does in the classroom when disciplining disruptive students?

R: No. If a student is disruptive in the class, that is, what the teacher claims as disruption, she cuts your grades. Since we take all our classes with the same teacher, this is not a good thing. This is why my math grades are so poor. I talk a lot in math because it makes me think. The teacher is boring and I just have to say something.

Q: In what ways are the classroom subjects that you are learning in your classroom useful in your life?

R: I can teach math in college, or I can become a mathematical engineer. Typing can be useful if one wants to become an editor, and reading can be useful as an after-school math tutor.

Patricia.

Q: Tell me what you think makes a good classroom teacher.

R: One who can explain math or other subjects where the students can understand without being confused even more by the teacher. One who will not listen to other teachers when describing students' behavior, saying students have behavior problems when, in reality, we are just bored to death because teachers teach the same subjects the same way over and over and we already know the stuff. We want to do work that will allow us to think and express ourselves so we can excel as other students attending Ivy League Schools. I read a lot and I have read about these students; they are smart and I know if I am given the same opportunity I can be just as smart or smarter. I want to be an attorney and I know the way we are taught, I won't be entering any college with high rating, unless I pass the SAT Test with a high score and that is what I'm banking on. I can study on my own. My aunt gives me points on how to study and I share them with my friends and anyone else who wants to study with me.

Q: What unique features do you, as a student, bring into your third- or sixth-grade classroom?

R: Math, science, and music. But, in science, we do not do experiments in class that I see students on televison participating in. Students are entering science fairs, presenting their projects to the nation, but my teacher says the school does not have funding for insurance to cover students at our school.

Q: Are there special things that your teacher does in the classroom when disciplining disruptive students?

R: No, nothing special, just a lot of treats and suspensions.

Q: In what ways are the classroom subjects that you are learning in your classroom useful in your life?

R: Math is useful for accounting and music, science is useful for inventions and medicine that is, advanced math and science.

Rosa.
Q. Tell me what you think makes a good classroom teacher.

R. A good teacher is one who can separate personal problems from professional ones. One who has respect for herself or himself as well as the students.

Q. What unique features do you, as a student, bring into your third- or sixth-grade classroom?

R. I'm an organizer, a leader, good in math and good with computers.

Q Are there special things that your teacher does in the classroom when disciplining disruptive students?

R. No.

Q. In what ways are the classroom subjects that you are learning in your classroom useful in your life?

R. All the subjects can be beneficial in our lives if they were taught so we can learn them and be able to compete with students who are doing advanced work.

Chama.    Q. Tell me what you think makes a good classroom teacher.

R. A good teacher is one who is non-critical toward students, but gives constructive criticism to students.

Q. What unique features do you, as a student, bring into your third- or sixth-grade classroom?

R. I have good leadership skills, I am good in math, science and sports.

Q. Are there special things that your teacher does in the classroom when disciplining disruptive students?

R. One time my kindergarten teacher gave me what I understand today is a pep talk to get me to eat that nasty cafeteria food; other than that, nothing.

Q. In what ways are the classroom subjects that you are learning in your classroom useful in your life?

R. Math might help me land a good job as a surveyor for the city; I might go for a job like that because I have never seen a Black surveyor in this town. I know I'm good in math; I can work problem that my teacher can't work, especially those problems that cause one to think. She has to look in the teacher's manual to show us how to work these types of problems. By that time, I already have the answer, but she wants me to set up an equation which to me does not make any sense when you can see the answer. The teacher wants you to do a lot of unnecessary writing when math is so easy to do. We spend about forty-five minutes doing one problem using an equation when I can work the problem out in less than five minutes using three to four steps.

Caranda.   Q. Tell me what you think makes a good classroom teacher.

R. I consider a good teacher is one who is sensitive to the students needs, maintains their personal hygiene and wears appropriate attire, wears shined shoes, has good teaching abilities, not threatening to suspend students from school for nothing.

Q. What unique features do you, as a student, bring to your third- or sixth grade classroom?

R I'm a good at reading maps, I like geography and health.

Q Are there special things that your teacher does in the classroom when disciplining disruptive students?

R. No, all teachers do in this school is yell at the top of their lungs and threaten to suspend students for talking low. We don't talk loud like they do when they get together, and this is in the cafeteria, not in the classroom.

Q. In what ways are the classroom subjects that you are learning in your classroom useful in your life?

R. The study of geography can be helpful when one seeks for employment as a forest ranger, bus driver, study rocks, ship navigator, air line pilot, engineer, aviator or any other employment relating to the outdoors where water or the atmosphere is concerned.

Tara.

Q. Tell me what you think makes a good classroom teacher.

R. One who tries to understand the culture of other students, one who allows students to work together when she or he (because I have had a man teacher who really had an attitude toward students when the students didn't understand) cannot explain a math problem with clarity so all students can understand, one who can admit that she or he does not know everything, and who is able to direct students to other resources where the answer or answers can be found.

Q. What unique features do you, as a student, bring into your third- or sixth-grade classroom?

R. I'm a good leader, I have good leadership skills, I'm good in math.

Q. Are there special things that your teacher does in the classroom when disciplining disruptive students?

R No. Nothing special.

Q In what ways are the classroom subjects that you are learning in your classroom useful in your life?

R I want to be a math teacher and, with my leadership abilities, I can become a school's superintendent.

Noly.

Q. Tell me what you think makes a good classroom teacher.

R. I heard many of my schoolmates say that they think a good teacher is nice. Does nice teach you how to pass a test? Does nice teach you how to study? Does nice teacher teach students advanced work? These answers are "no." Nice in this school has nothing to do with educating us Black students. Some students think a good teacher is fair; I don't think so. If a teacher is fair, that teacher would be fair and honest to teach and not cheat us out of an education. This is what is going on at this school. We are being cheated and trained. To be trained, one does not have to think; in this school, we are being trained. If we were being taught, we would be given the opportunity to think, we would be learning how to make decisions and be prepared for higher levels of studies. Every morning I come a school where teachers stand before us with nothing in mind to do that will prepare students for the future; they go over the same materials day in and day out. I know how to read out a second grade reader and I know how to do simple math. I'm in the six grade and I know what I want to study. I was to have materials that are competitive, subjects that will enhance my ability to compete with other students who attend good schools and, if anyone cared, we would have these materials in this school. Everything I learned, I learned it without the help of any teacher in this school. The work in this school is far too easy for me as well as a for other students too; we don't say anything because no one will listen to us, we are bored. A good teacher is one who does not embarrass students if the students have a learning problem, one who teaches students and not train students, one who respects students, one who does not come to school smelling like alcoholic liquor or have a storage of pills in their desk drawer, and one who is well-educated to teach students with different cultures. I think a good teacher should be concerned about how students express their thoughts so that these students will become good students in the future.

Q. What unique features do you, as a student, bring into your third or sixth-grade classroom?

R. As a sixth-grade student, self-expression is one of my unique features. As long as I attend public schools, I will never be able to exercise my other good features. I have good insight concerning my future and one thing I am sure of is that I am not being educated, I'm being trained.

Q. Are there special things that your teacher does in the classroom when disciplining disruptive students?

R. No, not as far as I am concerned. If teachers think pulling cards is special or sending students to the principal' office, then that's special for them. But, as for me, I think it is a waste of time, a waste of good energy.

Q. In what ways are the classroom subjects that you are learning in your classroom useful in your life?

R. If I quit school at the six grade level and have children, I'll teach them how to read from a second grade reader; I can teach my children to read when they attend Head-Start. In this school we are taught to fail. The only thing we being educated for are to become dependable citizens living on the crumbs of society. You would think that someone had this in mind when teachers come in this school to train rather than to teach.

Salient points were addressed by a number of teachers who stated that the majority of their students were very bright and that it was the school's curriculum that was the obstacle in the academic failure of the students at the elementary level in general.

By interviewing teachers and students, there seemed to be some inconsistency in what the two separate subjects were stating concerning the extent between what teachers implemented and what students perceived being implemented from the school's curriculum. For example, teachers were stating in record numbers that students were coming to school to learn and were learning even though they followed the school's curriculum; on the other hand, students were stating that they were not being taught by teachers and they were failing. For example, students were dissatisfied with the way teachers implemented materials in the classrooms from the school curriculum. They were aware of the fact that they were not being taught to acquire a quality education. Furthermore, they stated, "We are treated by many of the teachers as if we were not human at the elementary level. We come to school to learn and are expect to learn; many teachers are failing badly in the area of teaching us."

# CHAPTER XI

# DISCUSSION, RECOMMENDATIONS, AND CONCLUSION

## Discussion

This chapter presents the discussion, recommendations, and conclusion. The target population for this study included sub-sample No. 1, consisting of 436 students who responded to the student survey. Of the 436 students, 132 were from one elementary school in Illinois and 304 were from six elementary schools in Mississippi. Sub-sample No. 2 consisted of 21 elementary school educators in Illinois and Mississippi. They responded to the 19-item teacher questionnaire. Of the 21 educators, 15 were teachers and 6 were administrators. In data analysis, percentages as well as means and standard deviations were computerized; T-tests and ANOVA were conducted for comparison and descriptive analysis. Comments and recommendations reported to the open-ended questions were summarized, analyzed, and codified.

The detailed results of this study were reported by research questions and interview questions in Chapter IV. The following section is the discussion of the results for this study.

## Research Question 1

In what ways do teachers implement a school curriculum for their third- and sixth-grade classrooms?

Contributions from teacher interviews from both third- and sixth-grade levels indicated they had many different ways to implement their school curriculum, expressed during their interviews. Some teachers stated during their interviews that they used hidden curricula for academic success. The results are consistent with Good & Brophy (1971a) and (Kerman,1979) who reported that when students are perceived as failures at the elementary level, experiencing difficulties in their studies, teachers repeat or rephrase the question or gave a clue 67% of the time. However, according to the interviews from some of the students, many teachers use the watered-down curriculum, knowing all along that it was designed to fail.

There is an insufficiency of teachers implementing a school curriculum for their third- and sixth-grade classroom. Inner-city teachers gave more directions, criticized their students more, asked fewer question, and accepted or clarified students' ideas less frequently. Behavior of these teachers related negatively to students from lower-socioeconomic backgrounds. Perkins (1985) confirms that students from the inner-city fail at the elementary level which related to withdrawal on the part of the student and criticism on the part of the teacher. In contrast, many teachers indicated that they were least prepared to teach because the school curriculum was designed to fail students from lower-socioeconomic backgrounds (Kunjufu, 1985). These results are consistent with the studies of Comer (1989) and Frisby (1992) showing that teachers implement a school curriculum in an unproductive manner. Good & Dembo (1973) found that 93% of teachers called students from lower-socioeconomic backgrounds to answer questions that required them only to recall information. In this study, students were given few opportunities to practice higher-level thinking. Bloom (1984) and Tractenberg (1974) stated that textbooks emphasize specific content to be remembered and give students little opportunity to use higher-level skills, such as giving opinions, assessing facts, drawing implications, and evaluating information or facts. But, according to the answers to the survey questionnaire and the answers from the interviews with students, there were discrepancies concerning the perceptions on the part of teachers.

Descriptive statistics for this study were computed to determine the means and standard deviation for 19 items measuring students' perceptions of teacher implementation. The means for students' responses for all 19 items of the student survey ranged from neutral to agree. The highest mean, 4.95 on a 5-point scale, for teacher responses, was significant for both items 4 and 6. Teachers strongly agreed that they did whatever questions 4 and 6 measured. The second highest mean of 4.90 was significant for items 2, 14, 17, and 3. Item 6 was the response with the lowest mean of 4.14. Teachers responded that they strongly agree with item 6 of the teacher questionnaire. Although item 6 had the lowest mean, teachers responded on average that they agreed with the statement. For teacher perceptions, perhaps these are tasks that they still cannot accomplish in their classroom teaching of students from lower-socioeconomic backgrounds (Anderson, Johnson, & Lang 1969).

## Research Question2

In what ways do the third- and sixth-grade level elementary students perceive what their teachers implement from the school curriculum contributes to them in the classroom?

One male student expressed his feelings toward his teacher. He stated, "I'm a good reader, I have a good relationship with my peers, I type and I'm good in math. Although my grades are very poor, this doesn't bother me because I have a mother who has faith in me and I have faith in myself. When I go to high school my grades will improve. My teacher just does not like me because she knows I'm good in math; she wants to kills my spirit, but she will never do that."

A sixth-grade male student said, "My math skills might help me land a good job as a surveyor for the city. I might go for a job like that because I have never seem a Black surveyor in this town. I know I'm good in math because one has to think. She has to look in the teacher's manual to show us how to work these types of problems and by the time she explains the first problem, I have worked out about three of them. I already have the answers, but she wants me to set up an equation which to me does not make any sense when you can see the answer. The teacher wants you to do a lot of unnecessary writing when math is easy to do. We spend forty-five minutes doing one problem using an equation when I can work the problem out in less than five minutes using three or four steps."

A female third-grader expressed her feeling concerning how she is treated in her classroom. She stated, "There are no special things that my teacher does for me for school success; all my teacher does is yell at the top of her lungs and threaten to suspend students for talking loud. We don't talk loud like they do when they get together and this is in the cafeteria, not in the classroom."

Another female student expressed her experience as a sixth-grade student. She stated, "I have heard many of my schoolmates say that they think a good teacher is nice. Does nice teach students advanced work? Does nice teach you how to study?

The answer to these questions is 'no.' Nice in this school has nothing to do with educating us Black students. Some students think a good teacher is fair; I don't think so. If a teacher is fair, that teacher would be fair and honest to teach and not cheat us out of an education. This is what is going on at this school. We are being cheated and trained. To be trained, one does not have to think. In this school, we are being trained. If we as students were being taught, we would be given the opportunity to think; we as students would be learning how to make decisions and be prepared for higher levels of studies."

"Every morning, I come to a school where teachers stand before us students with nothing in mind to do that will prepare students for the future; they go over the same materials day in and day out. I know how to read out of a second-grade reader and I know how to do simple math. I'm in the sixth grade and I know what I want to study. I want to have materials that are competitive, subjects that will enhance my ability to compete with other students who attend good schools and, if anyone cared, we would have the same materials in this school. Everything I have learned, I learned without the help of any of my teacher. A good teacher is concerned about her students in general and allows students to express their thoughts so that students will become good students in the future.

A T-test was performed for all 19 items of the student survey to determine in what ways third- and sixth-grade level elementary students perceive that what their teachers implement from the school curriculum contributes to their academic success in school.

Third- and sixth-grade students differed in their responses to items 9, 10, 13, 14, 15, 16, 18, and 19. Relative to the differences for items 19 and 18, third graders responded less favorably to the items. Their measures were 2.77 and

2.93, respectively, with T-scores of -3.62 and -4.54 at p =.00. Sixth graders had a mean of 3.42 for both items 19 and 18. For items 14 and 16, third graders also reported means less than neutral 2.90 and 2.96, while sixth graders reported means higher than 3.42. According to Miller (1988) effective teaching depends on effective communication. Teachers must be aware of nonverbal communication in the classroom so they can become better receivers of students' positive signals that reinforce learning. They must become more adept at avoiding negative signals that stifle learning. Teachers give more negative nonverbal feedback to "nonbloomers" than "bloomers" and twice as much praise to "bloomers" according to Vav Oudenhoven, Pieter & Siero (1985).

## Research Question 3

To what extent is the difference between what the teachers implement, and what students perceive as being implemented, representative of school curricula in third- and sixth-grade level classroom settings.

There are many teachers who view students as an entity for learning. They know that students do not learn by osmosis. It requires hard work, boring work without any shortcuts. It is drills and more drills. It is repetition and memorization. Students must learn how to read.

They must learn how to unlock words. They must recite long lists of words that have the same "a" sound as in apple, the same short "i" sound as in Indian and it, the short sound of "u" as in umbrella, the short sound as of "o" as in ostrich, or the sound of short "e" as in Eskimo. But how many teachers have the opportunity to take this kind of time to teach African-American and Caucasian-American students from lower-socioeconomic backgrounds who attend school in the inner-city? In this study, they had ample opportunity to take the necessary time to teach African-American and Caucasian-American students from lower-socioeconomic backgrounds. The results are consistent with the study of the ghetto education.

Rist (1970) observed the same group of students in the third grade, fifth and sixth grades in an attempt to discover how teacher expectations were formed. He concluded that teacher evaluation commenced immediately upon the student's enrollment at the elementary level and that teachers behaved differentially in terms of that evaluation.

Supporting his conclusion were observations. Within a few days, only a certain group of the students were being called upon to lead the class in the Pledge of Allegiance, to read the weather calendar, and to participate in show-and -tell.

In another study, "Pygmalion Black and white," Rubovits and Maehr (1973) observed teacher behavior following the manipulation of expectancy regarding student potential. As in previous studies by these authors, teachers gave preferential treatment to "gifted" students.

Additionally, to some extent, it depended on the race and socioeconomic background of the students.

## Research Question 4

To what extent do teachers implement their instructional strategies for African-American and Caucasian-American students from lower-socioeconomic backgrounds at the third- and sixth-grade levels for academic success in schools in Illinois and Mississippi?

Results of the study reveal that students from the two states are capable to excel if teachers would set aside their prejudices against those who are from lower-socioeconomic backgrounds and race. Those of lower socioeconomic backgrounds can learn just as well as other students from middle and upper status if teachers use instructional strategies from the curriculum that are conducive to learning. Many teachers have ways of implementing personal behavior and instructional strategies when it comes to describing students from certain geographical areas in the inner-city. Caste and class, relating to education, constitute one of the most blatant forms of prejudice in the educational system.

This is exemplified in the teaching instructional strategies implemented to these students.

In a study by Gouldner (1995), African-American and Caucasian-American students attending inner-city elementary schools were observed for one school year. Gouldner heard many elementary teachers complain about the students' lack of interest in academic success, belligerence, and disruptive behavior. She was prepared to see instances of abusive behavior—hitting, pulling, throwing, defense, and loud talking. When Gouldner and her colleagues observed the classroom, however, they rarely saw students misbehave in ways that matched the teachers' prior description. Instead, the researchers saw students getting out of their seats, wandering around the room, opening drawers, rattling paper, leaning across the table, and talking with other students, students calling out to get the teacher's attention, and turning toward or touching another student. These minor student disruptions, which were associated with the teacher's lack of management skills, occurred when students were unoccupied, when they made transitions to other periods, and when they became bored with drawn-out sessions. These things did not occur because the students were not uncontrollable, incapable of or unwilling to learn.

## Research Questions Relative to Teachers' Perceptions Based on the Grade Level

A T-test was performed in order to determine the differences between third- and sixth-grade teachers' perceptions. The results of the T-tests revealed that significant differences existed for items 8, 10, and 15. While the third-grade teachers reported means of 5.00 for the three items, the means from sixth-grade teachers were considerably lower. For item 8 (3.86), for item 10 (3.88), and for item 15 (4.63). Third-grade students were lower than sixth-grade on items identified in T-test tables. However, third-grade teachers reported higher means for items aforementioned. Significant differences exist for items 7, 8, 10, 13, 15, 17, 18, and 19 based upon location of the students. Significant differences also existed for items 5, 6, 7, 9,15, and 28 based upon location of teachers.

## Recommendations

Based upon this research study, with supportive evidence from other research studies, the following recommendations are offered to teachers:

1. Additional investigations are needed for teachers to learn more about instructional strategies used in the classrooms for academic success at elementary level for students from lower-socioeconomic backgrounds.
2. The use of survey questionnaires when it comes to investigation students at the elementary level in inner-city schools and direct observations and interviews are two major instruments that can be used for such delicate research.
3. Qualitative research is needed to investigate internship for novice teachers.
4. All curricula should be conducive to learning and contain cultures of all students from lower-socioeconomic backgrounds.
5. Qualitative research is needed to learn more about colleges and universities that prepare teachers who are studying to teach students from lower-socioeconomic backgrounds.
6. Encourage and provide opportunities for beginning future teachers to teach students from lower-socioeconomic backgrounds.
7. Monitor teacher interactions so that they are equally distributed among all students from lower-socioeconomic backgrounds.
8. Do not allow future teachers to graduate unless they have personally experienced the lifestyle of students from lower-socioeconomic backgrounds; this means live and teach in the community.
9. Parents who are interest in how they can because involved in their child/or children's education, recommended reading, <u>By The Sweat of</u>

Their Brow, a book By Dr. Lucille Jordan Jackson. This book articulates how children are taught and treated by teachers and administrators.

# CONCLUSION

1. Based on the results of this study, overall, there is no statistically significant relationship between what third- and sixth-grade teachers implement in their classroom instructional strategies for their third- and sixth-grade students.
2. There is a statistically significant relationship between what teachers implement and what students perceive to be influential from their teachers' instructional strategies in the classrooms at the third- and sixth-grade levels.
3. There is an overall statistically significant relationship between race of students and their academic success along with what teachers implement and what students at the third- and sixth-grade levels perceive in the classrooms. However, the sample for Caucasian-American students was relatively smaller than that of African-American students.
4. There are no statistically significant differences between female and male students at the third- and sixth-grade levels for academic success.
5. There are statistically significant differences between students' academic success among the students attending schools in the Midwestern and Southern portion of the United States.

*Dr. L. Jordan Jackson*

# REFERENCES

Adams, J. (1978). Visual and tactual integrating and cerebral dysfunction in children with disabilities. Journal of Learning Disabilities, 7, 197-204.

Amidon, E.& Simon, A. (1965). Teacher-pupil interaction. Review of Educational Research, 35, 130-139.

Anelauskas, W. (1999). Discovering America As It Is. Clarity Press, INC. Atlanta, Ga.

Anyon, J. (1981). Social class and hidden curriculum of work. In Curriculum and Instruction. Giroux, H. A., Penna, A. N., and Pinar, W. F. (Eds.). Berkeley: McCutchan Publishing. (317-41)

Babad, E. & Taylor, L. (1992). Transparency of teacher expectancies across language cultural boundaries. Journal of Educational Research, 86, 120-125.

Baldwin, J. (1987). The urban education. Journal of Negro education, 21. (241-247)

Bank (1966). Report of locus of control on the educational opportunity in the United States identified the black child's sense of powerlessness as they construct most significantly related to academic failure. Pattern (1973) includes that this deterministic orientation of locus of control underlies a moral inferiority, which impedes black children's success in education.

Bateson, G. (1972-80). Surps to ecology of mind. New York: Ballantine.

Baumeister, R. F., Boden, J. M., & Smart, L. Relation of threatened egotism to violence & aggression: The dark side of high self-esteem," Psychological Review, 103 (1).

Beacham, M. (1994). How good teachers make students believe in themselves. Executive Educator, 12, 16-25.

Beck, J. (1952). A study of international in racially imbalance. New York: Syracuse University Youth Development Center.

Bennett, C. I. (1990). Comprehensive multicultural education (2nd Ed). Boston: Allyn and Bacon.

Bennett, C.& Bennett, J. A. (1994). Teachers' attributions and beliefs in relation to gender and success of students. Paper presented at the meeting of American Educational Research Association, New Orleans, La. (Eric Document Reproduction Service No. 375127).

Billings, L. D. (1992). Culturally relevant teaching: The key to making multicultural education work. In <u>Research and Multicultural Education</u>. Grant, C.A. (Ed.) London: Falmer. (106-121)

Billings, G. (1992). <u>The dreamkeeper</u>. California: Jossey-Bass, Inc.

Billingsley, A. (1968). <u>Black families in White America</u>. Englewood Cliffs, N.J.: Prentice Hall.

Bloom B. S. (1956). <u>Taxonomy of educational objectives</u>. New York: Longmans: Greenland Company.

Boas, F. (1910). The race Problem. <u>The Crisis, 1</u>. (22-25)

Boas, F. (1911). <u>The man of primitives man</u>. New York: The MacMillan Company.

Bond, H. & Johnson, C. (1934, July). The investigation of racial differences prior to 1910. <u>The Journal of Negro Education, 3</u>. (328-339)

Bond, H. (1966). <u>The education of the Negro in the American social order</u>. New York: Octagon Books (Reprinted).

Boutte, G. (1990). Frustration of an African-American parent: A personal and professional account. <u>Phi Delta Kappan, 73</u> (100). (786-788).

Boykin, A. W. (1986). <u>The triple quandary and the school achievement of minority children</u>. Hillsdale, N.J.: Lawrence Erlbaum Associates. (57-92)

Brady, N. (1980). <u>The impact of compensatory education programs on equality of educational opportunity in desegregated elementary school</u>. Ph.D. Dissertation, Michigan State University.

Brophy, J. & Good,T. T. (1973). The teachers' communication of differential expectations for children's classroom performance. <u>Journal of Educational Psychology, 63.</u> (617-624).

Brophy, J. & Good, T. (1974). <u>Teacher student relationships: Cause and consequences</u>. New York: Holt, Rinehart and Winston.

Brown, B. & Louise, W. (1995). Educating the Black child. <u>The Journal of Negro Education, 3</u>. (241-245)

Buriel, R. (1978). Relationship of three field-dependence measurement to the reading and math achievement of Anglo American and Mexican American children. <u>Journal of Educational Psychology, 70</u>, (920). (167-174)

Campbell, C. P., Simpson, & Cooper, R. (1992). The self-fulling prophecy: Implications for the training learning process. (Eric Document Reproduction Service No. 35377).

Chas, A. (1977). The legacy of the social coast of the new scientific racism. New York: Alfred Knof.

Chun, W. (1987-88). Sexism in our schools: Training girls for failure. The Elementary School Journal, 85. (77-89)

Clerkson, J. (1983). Urban learning styles. In Children's Success in School, Lakebrink, J. M. (Ed.). Springfield, IL: Charles Thomas. (115-139)

Colman, J (1996). Equality education opportunity. Washington, D.C.: Department of Health, Education and Welfare, Office of Education.

Colwins, S. (1922). Principles underlying the construction and use of intelligence tests. In the Twenty-first Yearbook of the National Society for the Study of Education (NSSE), Intelligence Tests and Their Use. Bloomington, IL.: Public School Publishing Company. (43).

Comer, J. P. (1972). Black and White. New York: Quadrale Books, Inc.

Comer, J.P. (1989). Racism and the education of young children. Teacher College Record (3). (352-361)

Consortium for Policy Research in education (CPRE). Equity in education: Progress problems (CPRE) (Policy Brief). New Brunswick, N.J.

Daviderson, H. (1991). Children's perceptions of their teacher's feeling toward them related to self-perception, school achievement and behavior. Journal of Experience Education, 29. (107-118)

Delepit, L. (1993). The politics of literate discourse. In Freedom's Plow: Teaching in the Multicultural Classroom. New York: Routledger, Inc. (285-295)

Deutsche, M. (1964). A facilitating development in elementary school child social and psychological perspectives. Merrill-Palmer Quarterly, 10. (246-264)

Dewey, J. (1934). Art as experience. New York: Perigee.

Dornbush, S., Massey, G., & Scott, M. (1975). Racism without racism: Institutional racism in urban schools.

Duncan, G. (1993). Racism as a development mediator. Educational Form, 57, (4). (360-370)

Dunn, R. & Dunn, K.(1979, March). Learning styles practical applications of the research. Practical Applications of Research. Bloomington, Indiana: Phi Delta Kappas Center and Researcher, I, (3) (March 1979). (2-3)

Dunn, R. (1990). Cross-cultural differences in learning styles of elementary-age students from four ethnic backgrounds. Journal of Multicultural Counseling & Development, 18, (2). (68-93).

Edmonds, R. (1982). On school improvement. Educational Leadership, 40, 13-15.

Epstein, R.,& Komorita, S. (1971). Self-esteem, success, failure, and locus of control in Negro children. Development Psychology, 4, (1), 2-8.

Erickson, F. (1980). Fieldwork in educational research. Occasional Paper No.36. East Lansing: Michigan State University, Institute for Research on Teaching.

Erickson, F. (1986). Qualitative methods in research on teaching. In Handbook of Research on Teaching (3rd_ed.) Writterock, M.C. (Ed.) New York: MacMillan. (505-526)

Evan, D.& Alexander, S. (1970). Some psychological correlate of civil rights activity. Psychological Report, (26), 899-906.

Finn, J.D. (1982). Patterson in special education placement as revealed by the eds., placing black children in special education at the elementary level, 322-381. Washington, D.C.: National Academy Press.

Ford, D. (1982). Journal of Negro Education, 61. Howard University.

Frisby, C.L. (1992). Black children's perceptions of self: Implication for educators. Educational Form, 57, 146-156.

Gaertmer, S. (1976). Non-racial measure in attitude research: A focus on "liberals." In Toward the Elimination of Racism. Katz, P.A. (Ed.). New York: Pergamon. (183-211)

Gansneder,B. (1968). Student achievement. In A Report to the Columbus Board of Education, University of Ohio State. Cunningham, L.C.

Garrett, A. & Willough, R. (1972). Personal orientation and reactions to success and failure in urban black children. Development Psychology, 7, (1), 92.

Gavey, M. (1986). Message to the people. Dove, MA: The Majority Press.

Gibbs, T. (19880. Young, Black, and males in America. MA: Auburn House Publishing Company.

Goldenberg, C. (1992). The limits expectations: A case study on knowledge about teachers' expectancy effects. American Educational Research Journal, 29, 517-544.

Good, T. (1981). Teacher and student expectation. Midwestern. Educational Researchers, 6, (1), 7-17.

Grant, P. (1981). Using special education to destroy black boys. Negro Educational Review, 43, (1-2) 17-21.

Guttentag, M., & Klem, I (1976). The relationship between inner verus outer locus of control and achievement in black middle school children. Educational and Psychological Measurement, (36) 1101-1109.

Hale, J. (1993). Rejoinder to myths of black culture, learning styles. In Defense of Afrocentric. School Psychology Review, 22, (3) (558-5561).

Hamilton, R. Gingness (1993). The relationship of teacher attitudes to course implementation and students' response. Teaching and Teacher Education, (9), 193-204.

Heath, S. (1986). Sociocultural contexts of language development. In Beyond Language: Social and Cultural. Holt, D.D. (Ed.) In factors in schooling language minority students (143-186). Los Angeles: Evaluation, Dissemination and Assessment Center: Calif. State University.

Herskovits, M. (1958). The myths of the past. Boston: Beacon Press.

Hilliard. A.G. (1990). Misunderstanding and testing intelligent. In Access to Know. Goodal, J. I. & Keating, P. (Eds.).

Hoebin, A. J. (1954). A study of social status differentiation in the classroom behavior of nineteen third-grade teachers. Journal of Social Psychology, 39, 269-293.

Hollis, K., & Sarason, S. (1991). The relation of test anxiety and defensiveness to test and school performance in the elementary school years: A further longitudinal study. Monographs of the Society for Research in Child Development, 31, (2).

Hooks, b. (1990). Yearning, race, gender, and cultural politics. Henry. New York: Holt and Company.

Hurston, Z, (1931). Saving Black folk. New York: Library of Congress.

Irvin J. J. (1990). Black students and school failure: Policies, practices, and prescriptions. Westport, CT.: Greenwood Publishing Company Group.

Irvin, J. J. (1992). Making teaching education culturally responsive. In Diversity in Teacher Education. Dilworth, M. E., (Ed.). San Francisco: Jossey-Bass. (79-92).

Jones, F.C. (1981). A traditional model of educational excellence. Washington, DC: Howard University Press.

Kaufman, J. (1991). What puts public at risk? An analysis of classroom teachers' judgements of pupils' behavior. Remedial and Special Education, 12, (5), 7-16.

Keating, K. (1983). The hug therapy book. Minneapolis: Comp Care Publications.

Kehler, V. (1988). Teacher's briefs about at-risk students. Paper presented at the annual meeting of American Educational Research Reproduction Service NO. EdD 312-359.

Keneal, P., (1991). Teacher expectations as predictors of academic success. Journal of Social Psychology, 13, (2), 305-306.

Kleinfield, J. (1992). Learning styles and cultural. Fairbanks: University of Alaska Press.

Kowles, L. & Prewitt, K. (1969). Institutional racism in America, England. Englewood Cliffs, N J.: Prentice-Hall.

Kunjufu, J. (1985). Counting the conspiracy to destroy Black boys. Chicago: African American Image.

Labov, W. (1972). Language in the inner city. Philadelphia: University of Pennsylvania Press.

Lammereier, P. (1974). The urban Black family of the nineteen century: A study of black family structure in the Ohio Valley. 1850-1880. Journal of Marriage and the Family, (35), 440-456.

Laycock, M. (1991). Remembering Theresa: Please excuse me for doing nothing: I was just an observe. Teaching Education, 4, 33-39.

Lee, M. (1986). The match: Learning styles of Black children and microcomputer programing. Journal of Negro Education, 55, 78-90.

Lerner, B. (1972). Therapy in the ghetto: Political impotence and personal disintegration. Baltimore: Johns Hopkins University Press.

Lesniak, R. J., Lohman, E., & Churukian, G.A. (1972). Verbal behavior differences between inner city and suburban elementary teachers. Urban Education, (7), 41-48.

Letter, C.A. (1980). Cognitive profile: Basic determinant of academic achievement. Burlington, VT: Center for Cognitive Studies.

Long, H. (1934). The intelligence of color elementary pupils in Washington, D.C. Journal of Negro Education, 4, 205-222.

Long, H. (1935). Test results of third grade Negro children selected on the basic of socioeconomic status. Journal of Negro Education, 4, 192-212, 523-552.

Marcus, F. T. & Stickney, M. (1981). Color, class, personality. Washington, DC: American Council on Education.

Madhubuit, H. (1987). The Clash of Races. Chicago, IL: Lotus Press Inc.

McAllister, E. (1990). Issues in education, anatomy of a crushed spirit. Childhood Education, 66, 203-204.

McDermott, R. P. (1974). Achieving school failure: An anthropological approach to illiteracy and social stratification. In Education and Culture Process. Spindler, G.D. (Ed.) New York: Holt, Rinehart & Winston.

McDermott, R. P. (1977). School relations as contests for learning in school. Harvard Educational Review, 47, 298-313.

Messick, S. (1984). The nature of cognitive styles: Problems and promise in educational practice. Educational Review, 47, 298-313.

Miscel, W.(1966). Theory and research on the antecedents of self-imposed delay of reward. In Process in Experiment Personality Research, 3. B. (Ed.) New York: Academic Press.

Mullis, J. (1988). Theories for success. University of Illinois, Chicago.

O'Leary, K. D. & O'Leary, S. (1977). Classroom management: The successful use of behavior modification. New York: Pergamon Press.

Odum, H. (1910). Social and mental traits of the Negro. New York: Columbia University Press.

Ogbu, J. (1992). Minority education caste. Carnegie Council on Children Monograph. NY: Academic Press.

Perkins, H. (1985). Classroom behavior and underachievement. American Educational Research Journal, 2, 1-11

Pierce, C. (1974, June). The mundane extreme environment and its effects on learning. Paper presented at the National Institute of Education, Navy, Office of Research, Washington, D.C.

Possaint, A. & Atkisson, C. (1970). Black youth and motivation. Black Scholar, 1, 43-51.

Possaint, A. (1977, May). Ebony Magazine. Chicago, Illinois.

Rabinnowitz, R. (1978). Internal-external control experiences in black children of differing socioeconomic status. Psychological Reports 42, (3), 1339-1345.

Reiff, J. F. (1992). <u>Learning styles</u>. Washington, DC: National Education Association.

Reinert, H. (1976). One picture is worth a thousand words? Not necessary! <u>The Modern Language Journal, 60,</u> 160-168.

Reynolds, A. J. (1992). Early school of children at risk. <u>American Educational Research Journal, 28,</u> 392-422.

Richardson, T. Q. (1993). Black culture learning styles: Is it really a myth? <u>School Psychology Review 22, (3),</u> 562-67.

Rist, R. (1970). Student social class and teachers expectation. <u>Harvard Educational Review, 40,</u> 411-451.

Sadker, D.M. & Sadker, M.P. (1986). Sexism in the classroom: From grade school to graduate school. <u>Phi Delta Kappan, 67,</u> (7), 512-555.

Saracho, O. N. (1984). <u>Cognitive style and children's learning: Individual variation in cognitive process</u>. Urbana, IL: Eric Clearinghouse on Elementary and Early Childhood Education. (Eric Document Reproduction Service No. 247 034).

Sarson, S., Davidson, K., Lighthall, F., Waite, R., & Rurbush, B., (1960). <u>Anxiety in elementary school children.</u> New York: John Wiley Press.

Shade, B. J. (1982). Afro-American cognitive pattern. <u>A Review of the Research, 52,</u> (2). 219-244.

Shade, B.J. (1989a). Afro-American cognitive pattern: A review of the research. In <u>Culture, Style, and the Education Process</u>. Shade, B.J. (Ed.) 94-115,. Springfield, IL.

Shade B.J. (1989b). The influence of perceptual development on cognitive styles: Cross ethnic comparisons. <u>Early Child Development and Cares, 51,</u> 137-155.

Siddle, B.J. W. E. V. (1993). Interpersonal caring in the good segregated schooling of African-American children: Evidence from the research case of Casswell Country Training School. <u>Urbana Review, 25.</u> 63-77.

Sizemore, B.(1969). Separatism: A reality approach to inclusion. In Racial Crisis in American Education. Chicago: Follet Education Corporation.

Slavin, R.E. (1986) Cooperate learning: Apply contact theory in desegregated schools. <u>Journal of Social Issues, 41,</u> 41-62.

Smead, V.S. (1984). Self-fulfilling prophecies in the classroom: Dead end or promising beginning. <u>Alberta Journal of Educational Research, 30,</u> 145-156.

Smith, M. (1986). Meta-analysis of research on teacher expectations. Evaluation, 4, 53-55.

Stalling, J. A. (1990). Following through classroom observation evaluation. Menlo Park, CA: Stanford Research Institute Stanford Center for R&D in Teaching; Stanford, CA: Sanford University. (172-173)

Snowball, D. R. (1994). Thinking about language. Teaching Pre-K-8, 24, 64-65.

Stephen, W.& Kenny, J. (1975). An experimental study of interethnicity competition in segregated schools. Journal of School Psychology, 13, (3), 232-247.

Stronck, D. R. (1980). The educational implications of human individuality. American Biology Teacher, 42.

Swanson, L. (1980). Cognitive style, locus of control, and school achievement in learning-disabled females. Journal of Clinical Psychology, 36, (4), 964-967.

Swisher, K., & Deyhle, D. (1989). The styles of learning are different, but the teaching is just the same. Journal of Indian Education, [Special Issue], 1-13.

Talmadge, G. K., & Shearer, J. W. (1969). Relationship among learning styles, instructional methods and the nature of learning experiences. Psychology. Journal of Education 57, 222-230.

Tharp, R. G. (1989). Psychocultural variable and constants: Effects on teaching and learning in schools. American Psychologist, 44, (2), 349-359.

Tiedemann, J. (1989). Measurement of cognitive style: A critical review Educational Psychologist, 24, (30), 261-275.

Wapman, J. M. (1984). The Re-education of aphasic adults. Unpublished Doctoral Dissertation: University of Illinois, Chicago, Illinois.

Ward, W. (1986). Comment on Brown et al.":s" locus of control, sex role orientation, and self-concept in black and white third- and sixth-grade male female leaders in an urban community." Development Psychology.

Waxman, H.C., Wang, M.C., Linvall, C.M., & Anderson, K. A. (1988, February). Teacher roles observation schedule technical manual (Revised Edition). Philadelphia: Temple University, Center for Research in Human Development and Education.

Weber, B. J. (1994). The power of believing. Executive Educator, 16 (9), 35-38.

Williams, C. (1977). Destruction of Black civilization. Dubuque, IA: Kendall/Hunt Publishing Company.

Winfield, R. (1986). A study of social status differentiation in the classroom behavior nineteen third-grade teachers. Journal of Social Psychology, 39, 269-292.

Wright, B. (1986). Naturalistic in the learning process. Chicago: Third World Press.

Wright, B. (1987). The psychopathic racial personality. Chicago, IL: Third World Press.

Woodson, C.G. (1934-1969). Mis-education of the Negro, Washington, DC: The Associated Publisher Inc.

Wynn, C. (1992). Using decision-making activities with young learners. Georgia Social Science Journal, 23, 23-28.

Yarrow, R. (1958). Interpersonal dynamic in a desegregation process. Journal of Social Issues, 14, 3-63.

Young, R.E. (1996). Cognafective think. Louisiana: Press in the United States of American.

Zytkoskee, A., Strickland, B. & Watson, J. (1971). Delay of gratification and internal versus external control among adolescents of low socioeconomic status. Development Psychology, 4, 93-98.

# APPENDIX A

# DEFINITION OF TERMS

The following terms were defined for the purpose of the study:

African American—A person having origins in any of the black racial groups of African descent (Chinn & Hughes, 1987).

Culture—Changing values, traditions, social and political relationships, and a world view that is shared by a group of people bound together by several factors that could include a common history, geographic location, language, social class, and religion (Nieto, 1992).

Caucasian-American—A person having origins in any of the original population of Europe, North Africa, or the Middle East (Chinn & Hughes, 1987).

Learning style—The characteristics of students depicted most often through their behavior and personality as they attempt to begin, follow through, and complete a task (Dunn & Dunn, 1992).

Lower-Socioeconomic Backgrounds—Students who live with an income of less than $10,000 a year (Billingsley, 1968).

Liket-Scale—A Likert-scale is merely a selective form of questions seeking information concerning a given topic in search for particular information concerning a subject particular matter (Jordan-Jackson, 1999).

Cognitive Style—Cognitive style includes elements of implementations of students' developed modality of acquired knowledge which is effective and can be implemented to students with understanding (Jordan Jackson, 1998).

Life-adjustment Education—Teaching students how to think critically which includes Character education which teach and develop both mind and character of students (Jordan Jackson, 1999).

Heterogenous—A group of people who are said to be completely different as far as culture, color of skin, in some cases educational status, moral, and socioeconomic. In many cases African-American are the main target when it comes to diversity in a learning institution (Jordan Jackson, 1999).

Maturation—(maturity) a state of mind for students to develop for intellect in a learning institution, particularly at the pre-school and elementary level Jordan-Jackson (1999).

Modality Development—The stage of maturity where students are able to learn; there are three stages: reflexive, perceptual,and conceptual, all in this order. Not conceptual and then perceptual. This is the reason why students are confused at the early stages of learning. The reflexive stage, the infant makes use of his rapidly changing sensory capacities as they develop and mature, in an unconscious reactive manner. The second, or perceptual stage, the perceptual and mature level develops and matures without conscious awareness. Once the perceptual level has matured and developed, the child approaches consciously the third and final state—the conceptual level. At this level, students develop the ability to receive and integrate abstract stimuli with comprehension from a variety of modalities, associate the input with previous learning and express appropriate output signals (Wright, 1987).

Qualitative Research—a type of research which produces findings by using methods such as: interviews and observations to gain data which result in research experiences by the researcher. Qualitative research is a non-mathematical analytic procedure, (no numbers are used in the search. The findings are reported as found by the researcher, particularly in education by an earnest researcher (Jordan Jackson, 1999).

Quantitative Research—is a method of research that uncovers the nature and understand what lies behind any phenomenon about which little is known by of mathematical procedures(the use of numbers). These mathematical procedures can be misleading when it comes to educating children. Because the mathematical procedures can be altered to meet the need of the researcher (Jordan Jackson, 1999).

# ABOUT THE AUTHOR

Dr Lucille Jordan Jackson has an earned doctorate in Curriculum and Instructions. She is a professor of education, Behavior Counselor, writer, and researcher.

She is the author of one other book titled *By The Sweat Of Their Brow,* and now *Teaching Beyond The Limits.*

www.ingramcontent.com/pod-product-compliance
Lightning Source LLC
Chambersburg PA
CBHW021545290526
45785CB00004BA/1575